MW00449072

First Bites

First Bites

A **Science-Based** Guide to Nutrition for Baby's First **1,000 Days**

with more than 60 easy
recipes from **YUMI**

EVELYN RUSLI and
ARIANNA SCHIOLDAGER

Foreword by Anthony Porto, MD

Countryman Press

An Imprint of W. W. Norton & Company
Celebrating a Century of Independent Publishing

This book is intended to be a general information resource for expectant and new parents. It is not a substitute for individualized professional advice from your child's pediatrician or your own health care provider. The authors are not physicians or other health care providers and nothing contained in this book should be construed as medical advice.

Take your baby to the pediatrician regularly to make sure that they are meeting their growth and developmental milestones. Always consult your pediatrician (or take your child to the emergency room) if your child is sick or if your child appears to be reacting adversely to a particular food. If you choose to practice baby-led weaning, be aware that even small pieces of food may be choking hazards. *Never* leave an infant or toddler alone with food. Never give your infant or toddler vitamin supplements unless you are directed to do so by their pediatrician and consult your pediatrician about whether and when to feed your infant formula. Consult your own health care provider before ingesting or changing your diet to include significant amounts of any new food or supplements, especially if you are diabetic or suffer from an autoimmune or other health condition, if you are taking any prescription medication, if you are nursing, or if you have food or other allergies.

Any URLs displayed in this book link or refer to websites that existed as of press time. The publisher is not responsible for, and should not be deemed to endorse or recommend, any website other than its own or any app, product, program, or other content that it did not create. The authors, also, are not responsible for any third-party material.

Text copyright © 2023 by Evelyn Rusli and Angela Sutherland
Foreword © 2023 by Anthony Porto

Photos and section opener illustrations © Caer, Inc.
Badge icons starting on page 105: Muscles: Amin Yusifov / iStockphoto.com; Mama: PopsaArts / iStockphoto.com

For information about permission to reproduce selections from this book, write to Permissions, Countryman Press, 500 Fifth Avenue, New York, NY 10110

For information about special discounts for bulk purchases, please contact W. W. Norton Special Sales at specialsales@wwnorton.com or 800-233-4830

Manufacturing by TC Transcontinental
Book design by Allison Chi
Production manager: Devon Zahn

Countryman Press
www.countrymanpress.com

An imprint of W. W. Norton & Company, Inc.
500 Fifth Avenue, New York, NY 10110
www.wwnorton.com

978-1-68268-733-8

10 9 8 7 6 5 4 3 2 1

For all the babies,
today and tomorrow

Contents

Foreword

As parents, we want to do everything we can to ensure our children have the best start. The American Academy of Pediatrics has reinforced the importance of the first 1,000 days of life, beginning at conception through early toddlerhood, as the time when good nutrition is key for optimal growth and development.

As most parents do, I reflected on my own childhood when I became a new parent. I was a picky eater as a kid. I loved carbs, avoided most proteins, and of course loved sweets. My parents bribed me to eat protein or tried to hide it in my food. I knew it was there, though, and avoided their trickery. Not until my late teens did I change my diet and eat healthy. Many factors contributed to this prolonged picky-eating phase, but I wanted to do everything possible during my child's infancy to give him the building blocks for success.

Lucky—or not so lucky—for my kids, nutrition became my focus professionally, beginning in medical school. I earned my master's in public health with a concentration in obesity. After my training, I worked at a community hospital in New York and led its Childhood Obesity and Family Wellness Program. Then I switched focus to infant nutrition, realizing that primary prevention was the best way to address the obesity epidemic and to increase the number of healthy eaters. When I became a parent, I learned firsthand why parents have so many questions and realized that applying what I learned during medical school couldn't prepare me fully for the realities of parenthood.

Infant feeding has changed tremendously over the past few decades. How we introduce food looks vastly different from when I began my training, especially how and when to introduce high-allergy foods. Parents in my medical practice often ask questions about how to feed their infants: how to breastfeed, which formula is best, whether to use milk alternatives, when to start solids. The list goes on. Parents often Google these questions and more in the middle of the night. Health care professionals often give conflicting answers. Formula choices and the best way to feed my children overwhelmed me, too. I spent a lot of time researching the best bottle, the best first foods, and the milestones of infancy. Combining my medical education with the field knowledge I had gained, I cowrote *The Pediatrician's Guide to Feeding Babies and Toddlers* to provide parents with one trusted source to answer these questions.

Let's face it: Parenthood is amazing—and my 2 children have changed my life forever and given it new meaning—but we all are exhausted. I found myself making decisions while physically and mentally drained, especially in those first few years. When my daughter was born, she was colicky and vomited a lot. I often went to the local pharmacy at night, looking for remedies that I knew had minimal benefit, just to relieve her pain. In my state of exhaustion, I wanted to do anything to make her feel better.

Parenthood doesn't mean perfection. As a pediatric gastroenterologist, I strive to educate and provide plans for my patients so they feel empowered to execute them at home. What I didn't realize until I became a parent is that I should have acknowledged an unexpected reality: It's totally OK if some days aren't perfect as planned. It took becoming a parent for me to understand the reality versus the ideal.

My philosophy is that there's no one right way but rather a few guidelines to follow when feeding infants. Most important, within those guidelines, just have fun with it. I never want to be so prescriptive that I add to the stress of caring for a young child. When thinking about nutrition and introducing solids, remember these five points:

- Begin solids when your child is developmentally ready, typically around 4 to 6 months of life.
- Begin to offer high-allergy food consistently along with other foods after your child tolerates a few first foods.
- Offer a variety of foods that will help keep bowel movements regular by including "P" fruits such as prunes, pears, plums, and/or papaya into the diet.
- Avoid honey and foods with added salt until your child's first birthday.
- Avoid hard, cylindrical foods that can block a child's airway, such as nuts and whole grapes, and other choking hazards.

As I was becoming more involved in the world of infant nutrition, Yumi reached out to me to join their medical advisory board. I keenly remember the conversation with Evelyn. As she described the reasons behind starting Yumi, so much of what she said resonated with me. The company stands on a commitment to evidence-based science and a belief in the importance of providing certain nutrients during the first 1,000 days. Based on this knowledge and commitment, Yumi provides a well-thought-out plan to make it easier for you to offer solid foods that will start your infant on a successful feeding journey by introducing healthy foods with a variety of flavors and textures. This book gives you an inside view of the Yumi philosophy and the science behind the focus on the first 1,000 days. This information will help you understand the "why" in why you should be providing certain foods to your child during this key period.

More important, the book also gives you a step-by-step guide to how to do it. The recipes here are natural extensions of the Yumi brand, which seeks to ensure that infants and toddlers have key nutrients in their diet. For example, some of the dishes focus on iron and zinc, which become essential nutrients at 6 months for infants who are breastfed exclusively. The authors also understand picky eating. We all wish that our children would love what we put in front of them, but sometimes it takes time and patience. It's important to introduce foods early, but it can take 10 to 15 exposures before children accept new flavors or foods.

The authors know that each day we, as parents, are doing the best we can. Some days won't go as planned—remember, exhausted!—so this book arms you with the tools to give your child key nutrients that are designed to lead to a healthy lifestyle for your child later on. It provides information on maternal and infant nutrition and essential information on introducing solids whether you're starting with purées or baby-led weaning.

Having this book would have helped alleviate the guilt that I—a parent of 2 children, now 3 and 7—wasn't doing enough, and it would have armed me with what I could have done to make my children adventurous eaters. The recipes are simple to follow, and whether you're the parent of a toddler or infant or you're a parent-to-be, you'll enjoy this easy-to-read, evidence-based book on infant nutrition with a realistic perspective on modern parenting.

Enjoy each moment of parenthood because each is fleeting. My children have passed the toddler stage, and I wish I could freeze some moments (infant cuddles), while others I don't miss at all. (Bye bye, 3 AM feedings!) I hope you find this book helpful and that it gives you more freedom to treasure these truly special moments.

Happy eating!

Anthony Porto, MD, MPH,
associate chief of pediatric gastroenterology at Yale University

Preface

When I found out I was pregnant with my first child, I was, as any seasoned parent easily will recognize, a bit delusional. I was going to nail parenting. I had visions of speed-reading my way through every tome about it so I would know what to expect, expect better, and bring up all the bébés. Well, a funny thing happened on the way to the podium of the parenting Olympics: reality. Parenting is tough. A baby plops into your lap, and at the busiest point in your life you have to become an expert overnight on an encyclopedia's worth of topics. Even if you research and interview every new parent within a 30-mile radius, you still will feel like you're failing every day.

During the first months of parenting, I learned to adapt. I embraced the messiness that I was confusing for failure. I homed in on what I could impact. Nearly every sign pointed to nutrition. I didn't start as a nutrition buff, but I am forever a mathlete, a scientist at heart. My friends joke that I speak in data sets. So when I began learning about the importance of nutrition during the first years of life, I went straight to the numbers. I scraped every clinical study I could find, analyzing every number and percentage, organized it all in a folder, and did what every good mom does. I phoned a friend: my equally nerdy friend Evelyn Rusli. At the time, she was working at the *Wall Street Journal*. While not a parent yet, she became equally obsessed.

In the ensuing months, the folder became fatter. We dived into more studies related to the impact of first foods on taste preferences, the correlation of early iron to IQ, the evolution of gut biome diversity in year 1. I did market research at the grocery store, and the options in the baby-food aisle were appalling. In one dark bout of late-night research, I calculated the nutritional value of more than 100 organic squeeze pouches and found that 50 percent of their calories came from fructose. Even more distressing: many baby food products contain disturbing levels of heavy metals. Those epiphanies became the catalyst for Yumi. I gave notice to my firm, giving up a fancy title and a decade of climbing the corporate ladder. Evelyn broke the news to her Asian-immigrant parents (who, at the time of publication, still want her to apply to law school).

What started as "some research" has escalated. Three years after launching nationally, we were feeding 3 percent of all babies born in America and sending research to new parents every week. We picked up more nerds along the way. We brought on Michael Goran, an authority on childhood metabolic health; Josette Sheeran, the former executive director of the United Nations World Food Programme and a general badass who laid the groundwork for the organization's Nobel Peace Prize; the founders of Sweetgreen, who became friends and investors; and the other author of this book, Arianna Schioldager, an initial skeptic who now late-night panic-texts me about riboflavin.

What we put in that folder and what they put in this book will change you. You might not quit your job, but you probably won't look at a beet the same way again. Evelyn and I joke that anyone is just two factoids away from becoming a convert. You may be vaguely aware that nutrition is important. You may have heard all the clichés about food as medicine and you are what you eat, but learning about the power of specific nutrients during the first 1,000 days of life will reshape everything you thought you knew about food and parenting.

The goal isn't perfection. I'm eating french fries as I type this. The goal is to embolden you with knowledge so you appreciate the power you have during a time when you likely feel that you have little. The goal is to help you see the salad beyond the spinach leaves so you can make better choices *and* retain your sanity.

Angela Sutherland,
cofounder and CEO of Yumi

Introduction

"Begin at the beginning and go on till you come to the end."
—Lewis Carroll, *Alice's Adventures in Wonderland*

The first 1,000 days of life encompass the most profound period for a baby's nutrition and development. During the time between conception and age 2, a baby's brain, body, metabolism, and immune system all develop at superspeed. A baby's brain forms about 1,000 synapses by age 1. About 80 percent of what becomes the adult brain forms by the end of age 2.[1] During this time, 60 percent of a baby's caloric intake goes straight to brain development.

But let's back up for a moment because, *whoa*, that's a scary intro to raising another human. (Rest assured, we're here to hold your hand along this journey. You're going to need the help as you hold on to your butt and learn how to wipe your baby's.)

We've been trying to figure out how to feed our little ones for a very long time. Dubious practices litter the historical record. Chemical analysis of clay feeding vessels dating to around 2000 B.C.E. reveals the residue of animal milk. That doesn't sound surprising, but the use of porous, unfired clay vessels coupled with a lack of proper sanitation methods during this time likely made these vessels unsafe for kiddos. Parents and other caregivers in ancient Greece sometimes fed their babies wine and honey, both big no-nos. Wine because obviously—although the alcohol ironically made it safer to drink at times than frequently contaminated water—and honey because of the botulism risk, which we cover in Chapter 2. About 2,000 years ago, babies in India also imbibed diluted wine and soup.

Soranus, a Greek physician who lived around 98 to 138 C.E., helped pioneer both gynecology and pediatrics. Widely known among the ancient Romans as a big deal (and among recent generations for his snigger-worthy name), he used some, uh, *unique* methods to assess nutrition. For example, he advocated testing the quality of breast milk by placing a drop of it on a fingernail. When the finger moved, the milk was supposed to be viscous enough that it didn't run all over the surface of the nail. When the fingernail pointed downward, the milk wasn't supposed to be thick enough to cling to the nail. People used this criterion to evaluate breast milk for the next 1,500 years. All of which is to say, dear reader, that simply by picking up this book—and not living when wine was safer to drink than water—you're already ahead of the game.

A lot has changed since the days of Soranus. Fingernails no longer qualify as medical instruments. Also, an explosion in research on childhood nutrition has occurred in the past few decades. Progress has proven exponential, with a surge in data-driven insights in the period of life from conception to age 2. This period, known as the first 1,000 days, became popular just in the past two decades. If you take one point from this book, we hope it's the 1,000 days. (No need to take notes because we're going to mention it about 456 times between now and the index.)

Which brings us to the question implicit in the title of Part One of this book: what does it mean to build a healthier future? The first 1,000 days represent a critical window, a unique opportunity to change future health outcomes definitively. Failure to acknowledge the importance of this period has massive ramifications for individuals and society. Science has proven that neglecting it can impact our children's mental wellness and future success for decades to come in their educations, careers, social lives, and beyond.

In 2012, the Copenhagen Consensus Center, a not-for-profit think tank now based in Massachusetts, conducted a study on where to channel global aid to yield the greatest impact. Their answer: investing in childhood nutrition delivers the most bang for the buck, with a return on investment of $30 for every $1 spent.[2] Normally we don't think about investing in our babies in such cold, financial terms, but the point remains clear. Childhood nutrition matters enormously. That's why feeding our babies well can help build a healthier future in every sense of the phrase.

Everyone has a role to play, too. The power to change the status quo doesn't lie exclusively in the hands of policy wonks or the C-suites of multinational food conglomerates. That power also lies in our communities, in our homes, and that's where this book comes into play. It operates as an essential resource for parents looking to optimize time and to impact nutritional outcomes. It's for anyone who wants practical, science-backed information peppered with nerdy, sometimes offbeat humor and healthy, age-appropriate recipes with an eye toward nutrition and flavor.

We're excited to help empower you as you raise the next generation of healthy eaters who will appreciate, hopefully from an early age, that food serves as the foundation of our health, forms part of the fabric of our culture, and can be fun!

How to Use This Book

This book gives you a modern, approachable way to navigate vast amounts of scientific information. For time-strapped caregivers, we've split the book into two parts. You can read them sequentially, separately, or in reverse order. Jump around as you like; there's no wrong way to read this book.

Part One breaks down the details and importance of the first 1,000 days. Think of it as an inside-baseball look at your child's body with factual, relatable examples. At the top of each chapter in Part One, we give you a cheat sheet highlighting key takeaways to enhance digestibility. (Every food pun is intended 100 percent.) We want you to walk away from this part feeling galvanized to make educated decisions about food and nutrition.

In Part Two, you'll learn how to put that science into practice, but you don't need to have read Part One to reap the benefits. These nutritious, delicious recipes for mother and baby support you through pregnancy and guide you into your fourth trimester and beyond. Simple but nutritionally dense, they draw on the tenets of the Yumi Milestone Plan. This balanced menu helps babies get the vitamins and minerals they need to grow while also covering texture and taste bud training with scores of ingredients.

Many parents start solids with the idea that they can or must do it all themselves, quickly realizing that achieving good variety is hard. We don't want you to feel the need to do it all. Blending baby food is tedious. Knowing what ingredients to introduce when can feel nerve-racking. We've done the work for you—researching, collating, testing, feeding, and more—and this book removes the guesswork from the equation. Pick it up, read a bit, dog-ear your favorite pages, put it down. You don't have to read it all in one sitting, nor do you have to make every recipe in Part Two in one day—or maybe ever.

You're doing fantastic.

Now take a deep breath, hold on to your Soranus, and let's go!

Sweet Potato Latkes (page 229)

PART ONE

Building a Healthier Future

The First 1,000 Days

FROM SEED TO SAPIENT

CHEAT SHEET

In this chapter, we outline the science on food and a baby's development for the first 1,000 days, including:

- Why it's the most important period for nutrition and development
- The four key development areas that food impacts
- Why you don't need to panic

It's a common misconception that our DNA determines our fate, that the genetic contributions of our parents encode who we become. That's true but only partly. Epigenetics, meaning our behaviors and how we interact with our environment, can impact the expression of our genes. All sorts of factors can affect them: stress and exercise, for instance. Starting in the womb, food represents the number one environmental variable for babies.[1]

Long before we're even a twinkle in our parents' eyes, food influences our future. It starts as early as the health and diets of mother and father prior to conception. Studies suggest, for instance, that undernourished fathers who lack protein in their diets tend to have babies with a greater risk of metabolic health issues down the line.[3] But profound scientific consensus points to this specific window, from conception to age 2, as the most important period for nutrition and development. So you have a lot of power here. Food choices for yourself and your baby matter.

You might be reading this book as a type A, get-it-done planner. You love a good spreadsheet. You want to know what to expect and when to expect it. Congrats, you're a unicorn! If, like others of us, you've come to this information well past the point of conception, you're also a unicorn—a normal, human unicorn that's majestic but also eats in bed and is 100 percent OK with that. Our point is that the science around the first 1,000 days should guide you, not guilt you. Say it aloud if you need to: *guide, not guilt.*

FUN FACT

Babies' cells have an epigenetic "memory" of their neonatal exposures, or exposome, that persist throughout their lives.[2]

For a sanity check, let's go to the opposite end of the spectrum and look at the oldest recorded human ever to have lived. Jeanne Calment of Arles, France, holds the world record for longest life ever.[4] Born in 1875, she died in 1997 at 122 years 164 days old. She stands as a paradigm of longevity, bolstered by a spectrum of biological factors, but she made decisions throughout her life that contributed to that longevity, including:

- **MEDITATION.** She prayed every evening at her local church until age 108. When she moved to a retirement home, she prayed every morning.
- **MENTAL STIMULATION.** She played the piano, listened to the news, and stayed cerebrally active.
- **PHYSICAL ACTIVITY.** She rode a bicycle until age 100, climbed the stairs at St. Triomphe Church until age 108, and walked daily, no matter the weather.
- **REGULAR SLEEP.** Reports indicate that, at the retirement home, she slept from 10 PM to 6:45 AM and took a regular 2-hour nap in the afternoon.

The world's oldest supercentenarian ate a relatively healthy Mediterranean diet, with lots of olive oil and garlic. She also had only coffee for breakfast, ate chocolate after every meal, drank red wine, and smoked cigarettes after meals until age 117. That's when she decided it was time to quit. She did plenty right but a lot more wrong. Doctors would have told her to quit smoking a *century* before she did. The scientific world endlessly debates the benefits of dark chocolate as a source of antioxidants and red wine in heart-healthy moderation. Calment wasn't perfect, and the science surrounding the first 1,000 days didn't exist in 1885. Still, she lived a long, happy existence because she made choices throughout her life that affected her health outcomes.

What does that mean for you and your little one? It means that you're not screwed. You haven't ruined your baby. You're beginning a lifelong food journey for you and your sweet spawn.

The Window of Opportunity

We've reached an age of peak information. In America alone, more than 2 million blog posts go live, scientific journals publish more than 6,800 research papers, and publishers publish some 2,700 books—*every single day*. With every rotation of the earth, the total amount of data produced would fill a stack of books stretching to the moon and back. The love you have for your little one stretches just as far, so you want to read it all. But you can't, and you shouldn't. Like a diaper blowout, there's a lot of crap out there.

But there is clear consensus around the importance of the first 1,000 days. In the past decade, scientists and researchers have circled that period, from conception to age 2, as the most important time for nutrition in a person's life. In 2008, *The Lancet*, a prestigious British medical journal, published a landmark series on maternal and infant nutrition that established the concept. The report concluded that food consumed during this period has a lasting impact through adulthood and that nutrient deficiencies then can lead to "irreversible damage." The series caused seismic waves in the field of nutrition, dramatically influenced research, spurred governments to take notice, and shaped policy across the globe, ultimately giving rise to NGOs focused exclusively on that time frame. Our advisor and former head of the UN's World Food Programme, Josette Sheeran has spoken repeatedly about the irreversible nature of malnutrition during this narrow window, calling the lack of nutrition during this period the "gravest threat to public health," on par with climate crisis.

The concept can feel a bit intimidating, but think of it with an empowering, glass-half-full approach. In a stretch of time when you feel like you have no control, you have far more than you think. We've mined mountains of clinical studies and literature on this period into a little molehill for you in the form of this book. So let's break down food's impact during the 1,000 days into four key areas:

1
brain
development

2
physical
growth

3
metabolic
health and taste
preferences

4
gut biome and
immunity

As you can see already, every inch of your baby's body correlates directly to nutrition during this period. Consider it your kiddo's most important software upgrade. You're programming your little one's body to maximize a lifetime of health.

We realize that we're asking a lot of you, including rethinking your relationship to food. If you've tried to give up a specific food or worked at healthier lifestyle adjustments, you already know that it requires more than a simple shift in thinking. (The current estimate puts it at about 66 days for a new habit to form successfully.)[5] Every thought we have requires a physical change in our brain and more than just willpower. Numerous studies have found junk food, especially products containing large amounts of processed, refined sugars, to be highly addictive, potentially more than cocaine.[6] Thankfully babies act as amazing motivators and catalysts for change.

If you're reading this pregnant, you probably already are scrutinizing where you live, how you get around, and how you organize your time and life. Consider food another item on that list, one that can have far-reaching implications for your baby and your whole family's health. When in doubt, stay calm and keep old Jeanne Calment in mind.

Brain Development

Look at your kiddo, all giggles and farts, and you might think not much is going on upstairs, at least not yet. It turns out that the exact opposite holds true. Based on neural activity, your baby's brain is outfiring yours any day of the week. This mental plasticity has its roots in your child's incredible growth, happening right now.

Nowhere does that growth appear more dramatic than in their rapidly expanding brainmeats.

To understand how nutrition is impacting your baby's brain, we need to peer into the firestorm of activity happening inside that adorable noggin. In a short period of time, your baby's body is racing to build a whole brain. A lot of that work happens in utero, which is why prenatal vitamins are so important and why your ob-gyn will drone on about folate deficiencies and the risk of neural-tube defects. At birth, a baby's brain is about 25 percent of its adult size, while a baby's body is just 5 percent of its adult size. That little brain contains 100 billion neurons—almost all the neurons the brain will ever need—and it's making more than 1 million neural connections per second. It will double in size in about 90 days, eventually reaching nearly 80 percent of the adult brain by age 2.[7]

At this stage, your baby's brain is hyperconnected, with about 15,000 synapses per neuron, more than double the synapses in the adult brain. Over time, as the child matures, the brain learns which connections matter and which don't. It eventually prunes these connections (more on that later), but in these first years it's conducting a symphony of activity. The number one power source for all this activity is, you guessed it, food. What a child consumes during this window—through the umbilical cord, boob, bottle, or by hand—supports the explosive growth of gray matter. About 60 percent of everything your baby is consuming goes straight to brain development. Those first bites matter. They are the literal building blocks of brain matter.

Think of your baby's belly as a teeny fuel tank, which is exactly what it is. You want to cram as much top-notch fuel in that limited space. Pour in too much junk, like sugar and empty calories, and you'll limit your child's potential because your baby's brain won't get the essential building blocks such as healthy fats, protein, iron, and other key nutrients to build a proper brain.

This Is Your Brain on Food

We've heard about "brain food" forever, but what does it mean? Let's do a *Magic School Bus* take on the brain and dive in to neural development during the first 1,000 days of life.

The brain is the body's ultimate command center. It takes center stage during this golden window. Macronutrients, such as healthy fats and proteins, and micronutrients, including folate and iron, are enormously important to brain development. (Feel free to jump to our micro and macro breakdowns in Chapter 4). Folate helps close neural tubes early in a baby's development, and iron helps form hemoglobin, which carries oxygen to the brain.

Unfortunately, some of the most common deficiencies apply to these power nutrients. It's pretty common for babies to become iron deficient, especially after 6 months, when they've depleted the iron stores they had at birth. An estimated 40 percent of infants worldwide have an iron deficiency, and that number stretches beyond the developing world. Even in America, an estimated 1 in 5 kids receive an anemia diagnosis at some point.[8] Moreover, these deficiencies aren't confined to one part of the economy. Iron deficiencies occur across income levels.

Deficiencies during such a critical period create ripple effects throughout life. Scientists have shown that iron deficiencies impair physical and mental growth. In one key study, children treated for iron deficiency during infancy continued exhibiting cognitive issues, such as lower test scores, and behavioral issues, such as anxiety or depression, more than 10 years later. The study controlled for various background factors, making the results statistically significant, and it showed that even a dip in normal iron levels during the 1,000-day window could impact the brain.[9]

Most children in America aren't at risk for severe hunger, but the major problem of food insecurity disproportionately affects 40 percent of lower-income families nationally. In 2021, some 13 million children, roughly 1 in 6, experienced nutrient deficiencies linked to food insecurity that will lead to long-term effects, including low achievement in school, emotional problems, and poor health. According to one study of children under age 3 who experienced food insecurity, 90 percent were more likely to have fair or poor health than good or excellent health. The same study notes that 76 percent were more likely to have problems in cognitive, language, and behavioral development.[10] Meanwhile, what American children are eating when not eating nutritious foods further drags on their health, creating a double-whammy scenario. A 2002 study concluded that a diet high in fat and refined sugar reduces neural plasticity and learning. In this study, rats given this diet, typical of most industrialized Western societies—and, let's be real, especially America—exhibited reduced brain function, learning, and memory.[11]

All told, that adds up to a lot of brain cells. Medical experts estimate that resolving for iodine, iron, and zinc, just three common deficiencies, would raise the world's average IQ by 10 points.[12]

Oh, Behave

Brain food goes beyond IQ, though. What we eat also affects our moods and emotional and social development. For hard proof, look no further than the millions of #hangry posts on Instagram.

One study found that poor nutrition during preschool increases antisocial behavior during elementary school.[13] As you might expect, poor nutrition has a far-reaching effect on our command center. Evidence suggests that antisocial children are at risk for becoming antisocial adolescents and adults. Scientific research also suggests a connection between health behaviors and bullying. In a 2017 study, researchers found "that youths with low-quality diets incurred a 123 percent increase in the odds of attaining bully status, relative to youths with high-quality diets."[14] We're not going to take on bullying or antisocial behavior in this book, but the more we study the effects of food, the bigger the opportunity we have to improve future generations.

Physical Growth

How tall are you? You might think that your height was determined by the time you were born. If so, you'd be only half right. It's unlikely that a 5-foot man and a 5-foot woman will make a 6-foot 9-inch LeBron James, but at birth your adult height falls into a range. Evelyn, for instance, is 5 feet 4 inches, the average height of an adult woman in America, but she could have been a few inches taller or shorter, based on (you guessed it) what she ate during her first 1,000 days. Arianna falls on the shorter end of the range and is very upset by this discovery. Lack of nutrition for the brain equals lack of nutrition for the rest of the body. It all connects. The human body has two distinct growth periods: the first 1,000 days and right before puberty.[15] Experts consider the first window more important and the second an opportunity for "catch-up" growth. Still, they widely believe that no adolescent catching up can make up for fully severe deficiencies during the first 1,000 days. Of the nutrients that contribute to height, protein, vitamin D, and vitamin A are particularly important.

In developing countries, where many children don't have access to proper nutrition, stunting can prove prevalent. According to the United Nations, about 150 million children (roughly 1 in 4) under age 5 are stunted.[16] Emerging studies indicate that some remediation can happen during adolescence, but it largely seems irreversible. Stunting correlates with more sick days and general economic disadvantages.[17] Evidence also points to longer-lasting effects because stunting impacts the height of future generations.

Metabolic Health and Taste Preferences

Most people talk about metabolism in terms of weight. It's why we gain weight and why it can be harder to keep extra weight off. We know that it slows with age. We often don't think of metabolic health as a zone of development, but it's one of the most important. Metabolism encompasses the cellular system that produces energy from food and the environment to power everything in our bodies. Without a functioning metabolic system, we can't function. In this case, function follows food.

Metabolic health is how well we convert food into energy. Having good metabolic health involves the absence of metabolic disease and having certain metrics—waist circumference, blood pressure, blood sugar, cholesterol, and triglycerides—all within particular ranges. Nutrition in the first 1,000 days creates the ultimate baseline for metabolic health. It teaches a baby's body how to respond to blood sugar and can increase or decrease the risk for future metabolic disorders. Generally we're not fretting about a baby's waistline. But we will consider how prenatal and postnatal nutrition impacts blood sugar and the future risk for metabolic diseases, such as type 2 diabetes.

Here's how the system works. The pancreas produces insulin, which it releases to process food, break it down, and produce glucose, a type of sugar. As the glucose moves through the blood and into cells for energy and storage, it becomes blood glucose or, more commonly, blood sugar. When blood sugar levels are normal, you and your baby are getting the energy you need to stay healthy.

In the womb, insulin doesn't cross the placenta, but blood sugar does. At around 13 weeks in utero, a baby will start producing insulin on its own. However, a mother's elevated blood sugar levels will prompt the baby's pancreas to make extra insulin. If it receives more energy than it needs, that excess becomes stored fat. Too much stored fat equals macrosomia, or fat baby. That's largely why doctors test pregnant mothers for gestational diabetes. For mothers, risk factors for gestational diabetes include being overweight prior to pregnancy, lack of physical activity, a history of diabetes in the family, and hormonal changes that can impact how the body processes sugar. Gestational diabetes can lead to pregnancy and delivery complications and make the mother more susceptible to type 2 diabetes down the line.

A baby exposed to too much blood sugar in the womb will be born with a pancreas on overdrive. It's used to producing a lot of insulin to deal with excess blood sugar. That situation can lead to postnatal problems because the pancreas will make too much insulin relative to blood sugar, leading to hypoglycemia, or low blood sugar levels.

Meanwhile, babies who don't get enough nutrition and energy in the womb become hyperefficient at metabolizing the energy they do receive. Unfortunately, if they receive significantly more nutrition and energy after birth, their bodies won't adjust to the overabundance, creating a postnatal spike in weight. Studies show that children who develop obesity early in life are more likely to be obese as adults and have a greater risk for heart disease, type 2 diabetes, cancer, and other illnesses later in life.[18]

As with most things, the Goldilocks approach works best. Too much or too little nutrition increases the likelihood that a child will develop metabolic diseases in the future, which makes intervention as early as possible—even before day one—all the more important.

A growing number of studies is digging in to the myriad ways that metabolism disruptions result in nutritional deficiencies. These studies look at changes in "energy, amino acid, and bile acid metabolism, the metabolic interactions between the gut microbiota and the host, and changes in metabolites associated with gut health"[19]—meaning our biochemical fate, which doesn't look so hot. About 88 percent of the entire American population suffers from some kind of metabolic issue.

As one of the wealthiest nations in the world, we've never eaten more food containing less nourishment. According to the Centers for Disease Control and Prevention (CDC), more than 14 million children—1 in 5 kids—are obese. Unfortunately, it doesn't get better from there. About 42 percent of the entire American population suffers from obesity.[20]

Metabolic health, part physical and also psychological, doesn't exist in a vacuum. It results from events, decisions, and habits that took place even generations earlier. From an emotional perspective, this 1,000-day period also proves critical because that's when we establish our relationships with food. Depending on your personality and body type, this point either states a convenient truth or comes as an unpleasant slap across the brain. Not only does eating well impact well-being today, but it also affects what you want to eat in the future.

The same goes for babies, who largely develop their tastes by age 4.[21] Everything children eat, through the umbilical cord or in the high chair, matters. According to Julie Mennella, PhD, a biopsychologist who has written extensively on the topic, "After the age of 3 to 4 years, reported dietary patterns/food habits remained quite stable, further highlighting the importance of getting children on the right track from the initial stages of learning to eat."

The Partnership for a Healthier America indicates that most young children fail to meet recommendations for vegetable intake. Only 10 percent of children consume the recommended amount. The organization considers this a "regrettable fact." Some more not-so-fun facts: Studies have shown that infants regularly exposed to sugar water prefer sweeter beverages as older children.[22] Similarly, infants who consume salty drinks and starchy foods high in sodium, such as heavily processed biscuits and crackers, prefer salty foods in preschool.[23]

Instead of treating food as just a nutritional source or something that just tastes good, think of it as a language capable of communicating with the body on a cellular level. If you serve your child our delicious Veggie Pasta Sauce (page 169), the vitamin C in the bell pepper provides immunity in a way that pasta, however tasty, can't.

If we start this communication early enough, our children's bodies will become fluent in optimal health outcomes.[24] Our little ones also will become familiar with the flavors of nutrient-dense foods. In the same way that it's easier to learn a language when younger, it's easier to eat healthily down the road if you start early. Setting those taste preferences at the beginning forms a massive piece of this proverbial pie.

Myth-Busting

Let's do a rapid-fire round of myth-busting. Don't feel bad if some or many of these come as a surprise. Many of us inherited well-intentioned but wonky fictions about kiddos and food.

Fiction	Fact
Food before 1 is just for fun.	**Strong taste preferences are forming during the first 1,000 days.**

You and your little one will have plenty of opportunities to play with food. We encourage it! It's fun to watch your baby's taste buds explode with discovery—again, big proponents of fun here—but food at this stage absolutely isn't *just* for fun. The development of taste buds during this period is only one of many reasons to take the 1,000 days seriously.

Fiction	Fact
Children get a pass to eat whatever they want as long as they eat veggies when older.	**Complementary feeding practices help prevent obesity later in life.**

This one crept into the diet zeitgeist and unfortunately has stuck around. In "Early Taste Experiences and Later Food Choices," a 2017 research paper, the authors note:

> the period of complementary feeding is also crucial, both for obesity prevention and for setting taste preferences and infant attitude towards food. Parents act by teaching children in different ways how, what, when, and how much to eat and by transmitting cultural and familial beliefs and practices surrounding food and eating. Parents' influence is significant: it is reflected both by what is on the plate and the context in which it is offered.

In short: what your baby eats now matters and how you set taste preferences matters because you matter.

An enormous amount of learning happens during a child's transition away from breast milk or formula. Taste predispositions, including the desire for sweet and salty, constrain that learning process. In this rare instance, youth isn't wasted on the young. Babies don't get a free pass. If they don't eat nutritionally balanced meals, they jump the fast track to health complications.

Fiction	Fact
Children don't have as many taste buds as adults.	**Newborns can have twice as many or more taste buds than adults and in more areas of the oral cavity.**

Do you know where we taste? (Hint: "mouth" isn't specific enough.) We don't taste with the underside of the tongue or the hard palate (behind your upper front teeth). We taste with the edges and top of the tongue, the soft palate (roof of the mouth toward the throat), and parts of the cheeks and pharynx (past the mouth but before the esophagus). You can remove or destroy all your taste buds—but seriously *don't!*—and most grow back fully in 2 weeks, making the taste organ one of the few in humans capable of total regeneration. According to "An Evolutionary Perspective on Food and Human Taste," this organ is "arguably the most durable and well-defended of all of our sensory systems, as indicated by the observation that humans who truly have no taste are exceedingly rare."

Why are we giving you this biology lesson? Remember, function follows food. This level of protection must have a reason. So which essential functions does taste serve for humans? Here's a great summary from that last scientific article:

> First, taste sensory inputs influence our thinking, deciding, and behavior toward sampled foods, both *consciously* and *unconsciously*, to guide ingestion. Second, taste inputs influence our physiology and the *metabolic processing* and *signaling* of nutrients and toxins once ingested. The former is involved with determining what foods enter our body and the latter with how these nutrients are handled once they enter it. Together these two functions help create our food preferences and feeding habits that sustain and maintain us throughout life and enable our species to reproduce.[25]

Those tiny little buds covering the tongue's surface really are our best friends. Without them, we might not be able to sustain life. Think about it this way: our proto-human nutritional needs and diet expanded around 4.4 million to 2.3 million years ago. Despite this expansion, we retained our preference for sugars and acids, which we need for existence. We crave fruit for the sugars they contain because our bodies naturally associate sweet with energy. Your natural love for sweets once served as an important survival tool. But to sustain life long term and to maintain its quality into old age, we need a lot more than just the sweet stuff.

Gut Biome and Immunity

As with the brain, your baby isn't born with a fully formed gut. Colonization happens (wait for it) in the first 2 years of life. Earlier, we learned that 80 percent of a person's brain forms during those first 1,000 days. Within the first 2½ years, the gut microbiome will resemble that of an adult as well. These two major developmental milestones go hand in hand, giving us the "gut-brain axis," a major determinant of future health.

The journey to a healthy gut starts the day a baby comes into the world. Birth itself provides the first milestone. The manner, whether vaginal or cesarean, impacts bacterial exposure and thus the colonization process. Later, the feeding journey—via breast or formula, then with solids—plays a pivotal role in continued colonization.

As soon as babies start breathing, eating, touching, and crawling, they're bringing all sorts of microorganisms, good and bad, into their bodies. Until about 6 months of age, they have an "open gut," meaning that whole proteins as well as pathogens can pass from the intestines directly into the bloodstream. Babies begin producing antibodies on their own around that time, when the gut closes. From birth to 6 months, bifidobacteria, which help digest milk sugars, dominate the gut. Environmental exposure and new foods increase the presence of other bacteria, such as Lachnospiraceae, Clostridiaceae, and Ruminococcaceae. Infants might have 100 kinds of bacteria in their guts. Adults, in contrast, have 1,000.

FUN FACT
Roughly 70 percent of the human immune system exists in the gut.

We are still unpacking the mysteries of the gut, but we know that food plays a key role in establishing and supporting its health. Whole-food ingredients, especially those high in fiber, help promote bacteria diversity. Having lots of good bacteria in the gut encourages neurological development and tightens the gut lining, which increases the absorption of nutrients. It also strengthens immunity. An imbalanced gut leaves the door open for digestive trouble, chronic illness, infection, and obesity.[26] It also can lead to common childhood issues such as colic, diarrhea, eczema, and food intolerances.

Medical experts increasingly advise caution with overusing antibiotics during this early period. Antibiotics can have a carpet-bomb effect, killing the good bacteria with the bad and impeding the proper colonization process. A 2017 study showed that the heavy use of antibiotics during this time correlated with behavioral difficulties, attention-span issues, and symptoms of depression years afterward.[27] Separate research further ties early use of antibiotics to an increased likelihood of allergies and obesity.[28] Antibiotics exist for a good reason, though, so, when your child is sick, *always* consult your pediatrician.

Conclusion

We truly are what we eat. As we have seen, the first years of food form the building blocks of our brains and bodies, shaping the road map of our future health. Every aspect of health ties to this period, and no one has more power to influence your baby's future than you. Today's nutritional choices have ripple effects on your child's physical abilities, resistance to or proclivity for disease, emotional and social development, IQ, and ultimately happiness.[29]

Now that we've established why all of this matters, let's dive into the how.

Nutrition

FOOD IS A VERB

CHEAT SHEET

In this chapter, we answer some of the most important questions about the nutritional needs of mothers and children, including:

- How to eat CLEAN
- Which nutrients mothers need while pregnant and lactating
- How to start solids and how to avoid the worst contaminants
- Whether sugar is as bad as we've heard

We live in a time of endless gimmicks and white noise, so first let's define "healthy." Every recommendation in this book ties to 1 of these 5 basic food principles:

Complete: Think about nutrition holistically, try to eat whole foods, and strive to hit the full array of micro- and macronutrients.

Low-glycemic impact: Always consider the blood-sugar impact of foods and their ratios of fiber to fructose.

Eat the rainbow: A variety of flavorful foods, especially vegetables, will help your child accept and enjoy healthy food in the future.

Avoid toxins: Pollutants, such as heavy metals, disproportionately impact babies, so focus on choices that minimize exposure.

Nutrient dense: Choose foods with high nutritional value and avoid empty calories.

The CLEAN acronym doesn't espouse a fad diet, nor is it rocket science. These easy guidelines reflect the areas of strongest consensus in the scientific and medical communities. But most families struggle even with these basics. For decades, industrial food conglomerates have pushed processed foods—highly profitable, highly addictive—at us. Food habits don't form on the first day of solids, either. They stretch back generations: "My grandmother fed this to my mother, and my mother fed it to me." Those patterns are tough to break overnight, but you already know the strength of your love for your child. We can't change the past, so let's start with pregnancy.

Days 0 to 280: What to Eat When You're Expecting

When I, Arianna, was pregnant with my daughter, I had miserable morning sickness, noon sickness, and night sickness. I woke up nauseated. All day long, sitting at my desk, I felt nauseated. I went to bed feeling nauseated. Only bagels helped. Why, I don't know, but they did. Bagels, delicious as they are, have little nutritional value, especially as a sole food group, but I didn't care. I needed to make it to my desk by 9 AM, and bagels got me there.

> "The doctor put me on a new diet plan, so I'm eating only bagels and doughnuts now. He told me to eat *hole* foods!"

What I didn't realize was that, as I neglected my nutrition, I was neglecting the nutrition of my fetus, bringing new meaning to "like mother, like daughter." Her development had started already. Her brain was forming. Around day 40 in utero, the first electrical brain activity begins. What a mother eats while pregnant can have long-term effects on the baby's development and behavior later in life, including the child's food choices and body weight. I had eaten myself into a bagel black hole, but you don't have to.

We have no control over certain areas of life: the weather, traffic, and the time that Apple loaded a U2 album on our iPhones. Luckily, you're in charge of your body, and you choose which nutrients to upload and which to power down. Food is the sum of its parts. Depending on which foods you're pulling from the shelves, those parts contain vital nutrients or no nutritional value at all. Expectant eating isn't easy, we know. Endless messages offer conflicting advice about what to consume during pregnancy. Plus, those nutrition labels do us dirty at times.

Label It

It might feel like it's been around forever, but the nutrition facts panel first appeared on the packaging of American food in 1994. Since then, it hasn't changed much, undergoing just three major changes: the addition of trans fat information in 2006; a new line item for added sugars, proposed in 2016; and listings for several essential vitamins and nutrients—including vitamins A, C, and D, calcium, iron, and potassium—also proposed in 2016. We say "proposed" because identifying those added sugars and essential nutrients didn't become a legal requirement for all manufacturers until January 1, 2021. In other words, our nutrition labels typically take a long time to catch up to the science.

If you're wondering why we don't cite federal regulations or current guidance on nutrition labels, that's because it would bore you to sleep, and you deserve a lot more than what appears on nutrition labels today.

Is coffee OK? What about spicy foods? Deli meats, raw fish, soft cheeses—the list feels endless, limiting, and hard to parse, all at the same time. Many pregnant women, especially those subject to nausea and hormone-driven cravings, experience a profound shift in their relationships with food. Varying factors affect appetite (such as Ari's bagel binge), limit essential nutrients (not bagels), and can lead to overconsuming unhealthy foods (more bagels). You don't have to eat perfect—meaning you can eat bagels—but remain mindful of the other nutrients you need.

Your Baby Is What You Eat

Over the past century, research exploring maternal behavior during pregnancy, especially in terms of food, has moved beyond old wives' tales to scientific recommendations about what expectant mothers should and shouldn't consume to promote optimal health for their babies and themselves. Much of it fixates on what not to eat, with endless hot takes on sushi, soft cheeses, and caffeine, so we're going to focus first on which nutrients are mission critical and what you *should* consume.

On average, a pregnant mother will need about 80,000 additional calories to make a new human, which includes whipping up everything from the placenta to those adorable eyeballs.[1] That works out to about 300 calories per day. The precise calorie count fluctuates as the baby develops, though. In the first trimester, you really don't need a surplus to your normal diet. In the second trimester, you need about 340 more, and by trimester three you should be gobbling an extra 450 calories per day.

Calories are just the starting point, however. It's also about the nutrients associated with those calories. You can consume all the calories and macros, such as protein, but if you neglect your micronutrients, you'll run into nutrition gaps. A 2006 study followed 45,000 Danish women who ate a standard Western diet, meaning lots of calories and protein but not a lot of vegetables. Their children on average had lower birth weights compared to the children of women who ate fewer calories but more veggies.[2]

The purposes of the following nutrients fall roughly into four basic categories: maternal health, antioxidants, DNA production and cell division, and brain development. During this period, the most important nutrients are:[3]

- **Choline** assists in cell division and the protective cover around nerve cells, making it critical for brain development.[4] (Low levels can lead to defects in the brain and spinal cord.[5])

- **Iodine**, essential for thyroid hormone production, impacts overall development and especially brain development. (Severe deficiency can cause pregnancy loss and infant mortality.[6])

- **Iron** is a big one. Mothers need about twice as much of it during pregnancy because their bodies are making more blood. Iron helps make hemoglobin, the protein in red blood cells. Many women suffer from anemia during pregnancy.

- **Omega-3 fatty acids**, important for eye and brain development, cannot be produced by your body, so you have to eat them. Evidence suggests that omega-3s can help prevent or lessen postpartum depression.[7]

- **Protein** breaks down into amino acids, which drive cell function, making it the ultimate building block of life.

- **Vitamin A** and other carotenoids power placental health, cellular differentiation, eye health, and the immune system. It's especially important during the third trimester, when needs are greater, and while breastfeeding.[8]

- **Vitamin B$_2$**, also known as riboflavin, plays a vital role in energy production and the development of bones, muscles, and nerves. (Pregnant women with insufficient B$_2$ have a greater risk for anemia and preeclampsia.[9])

- **Vitamin B$_6$**, also called pyridoxine, drives the production of serotonin and norepinephrine, two critical neurotransmitters.

- **Vitamin B$_9$** in its natural form in food is known as folate and in synthetic form as folic acid. It also helps form red blood cells and neural tubes in babies' brains.[10]

- **Vitamin B$_{12}$**, or cobalamin, promotes cell division and nervous system development.[11] (It pairs nicely with folic acid to prevent spina bifida and other defects.)

- **Vitamin D** assists in bone growth. (Deficiency increases the risk of pregnancy complications, including preeclampsia and diabetes, and can lead to stunting.)

- **Zinc** helps with DNA synthesis and tissue development.

Pregnant mothers need some of these nutrients, such as iron and vitamin B$_6$, in far greater quantities than normal. This handy table spells out exactly how much (picograms or milligrams) of which nutrients when.

Nutrient	Nonpregnant	Pregnant*	Lactating*
Folate (B$_9$; pg/d)	400	600	500
Iron (mg/d)	18	27	9
Niacin (mg/d)	14	18	17
Phosphorus (mg/d)	700	700	700
Riboflavin (B$_2$; mg/d)	1.1	1.4	1.6
Selenium (pg/d)	55	60	70
Thiamin (mg/d)	1.1	1.4	1.4
Vitamin A (pg/d)	700	770	1,300
Vitamin B$_6$ (mg/d)	1.3	1.9	2
Vitamin B$_{12}$ (pg/d)	2.4	2.6	2.8
Vitamin C (mg/d)	75	85	120
Vitamin D (pg/d)	5	15	15
Vitamin E (mg/d)	15	15	19
Vitamin K (pg/d)	90	90	90
Zinc (mg/d)	8	11	12

*Applies to women more than 18 years old[12]

Eat the Rainbow

By keeping your diet colorful, you can check every box easily.

RED
Anchovies (omega-3s)
Beets (folate, potassium, iron)
Fatty fish (B_{12}, D, iodine)
Liver (iron)
Raspberries (C)
Red bell peppers (A)

ORANGE
Apricots (A)
Butternut squash (A)
Carrots (A)
Mangoes (A, C)
Sweet potatoes (zinc)

YELLOW
Bananas (B_6)
Cheese (iodine)
Chickpeas (iron, zinc)
Eggs (choline, D)
Nutritional yeast (B_{12})

GREEN
Asparagus (folate, iron)
Avocado (B_2)
Broccoli (A, choline, folate)
Brussels sprouts (folate, iron)
Peas (A)
Pumpkin seeds (iron)
Seaweed (iodine)
Soybeans (choline, protein)
Spinach (B_2, folate, iron)

44

BLUE
Blackberries (manganese, C)
Blueberries (C, K)
Concord grapes (C)

PURPLE
Eggplants (manganese)
Dragon fruit (C, magnesium)
Plums (A, C)
Turnips (calcium, folate)

BROWN
Almonds (B_2, choline)
Beans (B_6, iron)
Chia seeds (omega-3s)
Flaxseed (omega-3s)
Hemp seeds (protein, zinc)

Lentils (iron, protein, zinc)
Mushrooms (B_2, choline, D)
Nuts (B_6)
Peanuts (protein)
Walnuts (omega-3s)
Wheat germ (choline)

WHITE
Cauliflower (choline)
Cheese (iodine)
Dairy (B_{12})
Fish (iodine)
Pumpkin seeds (iron)

The Not-So-Sweet Stuff

Early nutrition programming matters, and that also goes for overeating. Overeating during pregnancy and exposing a fetus to too many calories can put a child at greater risk for being overweight. Research suggests that women who gain excessive weight during pregnancy are more likely to have overweight babies. High birth weight correlates to future health complications, including chronic disease, even among otherwise healthy, full-term births.[15] In America, about 1 in 5 kids are obese by age 6; of those, about half were overweight by the 1,000-day mark.[16] If a child classifies as overweight at birth or exceeds the 95th percentile for weight to height, parents should track the child's progress closely and work with a pediatrician to help avoid future metabolic disorders.

When it comes to your child's metabolic health, one of the biggest variables you can control is sugar. One of our medical advisors, Michael Goran, professor of preventive medicine and pediatrics at the University of Southern California and codirector of the school's Diabetes and Obesity Research Institute, has looked extensively at the impact of sugar consumption during pregnancy and says it's clear that sugar, even artificial sweeteners, during pregnancy and throughout the first 1,000 days can dramatically increase a child's risk for metabolic issues. Studies show that a fructose-heavy diet leads to fructose in breast milk, increasing a child's chances of becoming overweight.[17] Drinking diet soda during pregnancy could *double* your child's chances of becoming overweight, an insight gleaned from a study of 3,000 pregnant mothers in Canada.[18]

During pregnancy, food programming is happening not just at the nutrient level but also at a sensory level. Overconsuming sweets during pregnancy impacts the mother's blood sugar levels and insulin production. It also primes the child to crave sugar later in life. We'll dive more into taste bud development in the next chapter, but the earliest flavor experiences, which occur in utero and during milk feedings, influence later food acceptance. If baby keeps spitting out veggie purée, *your* diet could be the reason.

A study showed that breastfed infants whose mothers consumed 300 milliliters of carrot juice 4 days per week during the third trimester or the first 2 months of lactation exhibited increased acceptance of carrot-flavored cereal.[19] The study also found that the mothers of infants exposed to carrot flavor in utero perceived them as enjoying the carrot cereal more than plain cereal. Infants in the control group, whose mothers drank only water during pregnancy and lactation, showed no such acceptance. This study demonstrates a relationship between food early in life and later food preferences, and it confirms the long-held belief that fetuses experience flavors transmitted from what mothers eat. According to the findings, breast milk and amniotic fluid contain flavors that reflect the foods and beverages that the mother consumes. This understanding establishes that "early flavor experiences may provide the foundation for cultural and ethnic differences in cuisine." We'll talk more about how this relates to food preferences in Chapter 3.

The carrot juice study marked the first clinical evidence that flavor experiences in utero influence a postnatal response. Another study found that garlic ingested by pregnant women alters the smell of the amniotic fluid.[20] Another stinky study found that infants born to mothers who ate anise showed a preference for the odor of the licorice-smelling plant. In contrast, children born to mamas who didn't eat anise showed neutral or aversion responses to it.

Fetuses experience flavors transmitted from what mothers eat.

One of the most influential studies on this topic took place in Guatemala from 1969 to 1977. In a longitudinal study, researchers at the Nutrition Institute of Central America and Panama examined the long-term effects of nutrition. During this period, pregnant women, lactating mothers, and children under age 7 in two villages received a high-quality supplement called atole, which contains protein and micronutrients. In two control villages, similar groups received a low-nutrient, sugary drink called fresco. Researchers assigned villagers to the groups at random. The results provided one of the first looks at the vulnerability of the first 1,000 days. Compared with fresco, atole improved total nutrient intake (protein, energy, micronutrients) and reduced stunting but only in children younger than age 3.[21]

Follow-up studies from 1988 to 2007 provided even more empirical science on the effects of nutrition, growth, and development. Researchers found that intelligence improved in atole villages but only in those who received the supplement before age 3. This data supports the idea of the 1,000 days as a golden window of opportunity and has influenced nutrition policy and other scientific studies.

> ## Smell + Taste = Flavor
>
> You can detect only five tastes: bitter, salty, savory, sour, and sweet. Anything beyond that counts as flavor and comes from the combination of taste and smell. Around 80 percent of flavor is smell, not taste. The olfactory bulb, the part of your brain that processes smells, connects to the amygdala and hippocampus, which handle emotions and memories, so at an anatomical level the smell of food can connect you mentally to certain places and people. That's why the olfactory sense can impart feelings of familiarity and comfort.
>
> Many studies confirm that children are more likely to choose foods in the future with which they already have had contact.[22] Want your kid to eat more kale and arugula? You need to do the same.

Days 281 to 462: Milking It

For those who boob it, breastfeeding is free and offers effectively complete nutrition for baby during the first sprint of life. The benefits of breastfeeding are well documented. Breast milk promotes sensory and cognitive development. It supports a healthy metabolism, self-regulation of appetite, and improved immune function in babies, preventing the length and severity of common childhood illnesses.[23]

FUN FACT

The composition of breast milk changes based on baby's growth and development. How cool is that?

It reduces a baby's risk of developing digestive or breathing issues, diabetes, obesity, and the likelihood of sudden infant death syndrome. Breast milk contains more than 50 immune factors and provides antibodies that reduce the likelihood of illness and allergic reactions before the gut closes. It also helps beneficial bacteria develop. Studies show that exclusive breastfeeding for roughly the first 6 months decreases the risk of respiratory and gastrointestinal infection.[24] Research also shows that every month of breastfeeding in the first year of life decreases the likelihood of obesity in childhood, adolescence, *and* adulthood.[25]

The benefits of breastfeeding extend to mothers as well. Hormone surges from breastfeeding support a mother's body as it heals from pregnancy and birth. It also aids in losing excess pregnancy weight and reducing the risk of breast cancer, ovarian cancer, type 2 diabetes, and cardiovascular disease.[26] The World Health Organization recommends breastfeeding exclusively until roughly 6 months of age, but for many reasons a mother might not be able to breastfeed, or a baby might need weaning before 6 months. Ultimately it's your call, and fed is best.

Lactation Considerations

You need to stay hydrated and consume additional food to support healthy milk production. You're looking at about 330 extra calories per day, depending on diet and activity level.[27]

Some of the nutrients that make their way into breast milk will come from your own stores. For instance, your body will pull calcium from your bones to ensure that your baby has enough. Bone loss during this period hovers near 5 percent.[28] Just like during pregnancy, maternal nutrition at this stage means maintaining your own health as well. Your body will prioritize your child's needs ahead of your own, which makes excellent guilt-trip fodder for arguing with your kid about curfew in 15 years.

The intense yellow color of colostrum, or breast milk produced immediately after birth, comes from a large concentration of carotenoids. During the colostrum period, which lasts about a week, the milk profile increases in fat and lactose, while protein and mineral concentrations decline.

In your diet, be mindful of beta-carotene (which converts to vitamin A in the body) and vitamins B_6, B_{12}, and D. When considering supplementation, don't overdo vitamin D because excess passes through breast milk to the baby. The fats in your diet will impact the fatty-acid profile of your breast milk, too, so eat plenty of whole foods high in omega-3s.[29] The American Academy of Pediatrics (AAP) suggests that breastfeeding mothers eat 200 to 300 milligrams of omega-3 fatty acids every day. If you eat fish for your healthy fats, focus on fish that are low in mercury and other heavy metals, such as anchovies, wild salmon, or sardines.

Also keep in mind that a couple of poor nutrition days won't kill the quality of your breast milk, either. The nutrient content of the milk doesn't change dramatically after brief, short-term drops in dietary intake.[30]

Your Milk-Making Menu

These nourishing foods will help your milk supply.

Almonds	Green papayas
Bananas	Legumes
Barley	Milk thistle
Beans	Oats
Brewer's yeast	Sweet potatoes
Dark greens	Water
Garlic	

Day 463ish: A Solid Start

Don't use your baby's weight or size as a gauge for when to start solids. Little ones vary *a lot*. Underweight babies shouldn't start sooner than 6 months, nor should overweight kiddos start later. The 6-month guideline comes from the maturity of the baby's digestive tract and developmental readiness. Gut biomes matter in babies drinking breast milk *or* formula. From birth to 4 months, a baby's digestive tract can't handle complex foods. Starting solids too early can lead to poor digestion, gas, or constipation. Nobody needs those farts or blowouts.

According to the AAP, an estimated 19 to 29 percent of infants are introduced to solids foods earlier than 4 months of age. In a study of 1,334 mothers, the most common reasons cited included: "perception of readiness, hunger, wanting to feed something in addition to breast milk or formula, perception of interest in solids, advice from a clinician, and to improve infant's sleep." However, other research suggests a link between introducing solids before 4 months and an increased risk for metabolic disorders.[31]

The most important health indicator is that the baby is gaining weight and growing. During these early months, babies exhibit an extrusion reflex, meaning their tongues naturally push out solids. In other words, follow your child's cues. Your little one may not be speaking, but there are signs to look for.

Signs That Baby Is Ready for Solids

WEIGHT GAIN: Roughly has doubled birth weight and likely weighs 13 pounds or more, according to the AAP.[32]

HEAD CONTROL: Exhibits good head control and can hold neck steady.

HIGHCHAIR-READY: Can sit in a highchair, feeding seat, or other infant seat without support.

EAGER TO EAT: Your baby reaches for food and shows increasing interest in what you're eating.

KEEPS FOODS IN: Keeps food in mouth rather than pushing it out with tongue (extrusion reflex).

ABLE TO SWALLOW: Can move food from front of mouth to back and swallow it.

In the beginning, breast milk or formula likely will continue providing most of your child's nutrition. Don't stress if your first feeding attempts end up on the floor. Embrace the mess. We humans have a hardwired predisposition for sweets, so many pediatricians recommend focusing on veggies as first foods. During this period, your infant is exploring the world of flavors and textures. It's a slow, experimental process. Start with just a few spoonfuls and allow your child to experience how it feels. Don't force the baby to finish anything, especially if your kiddo turning away from the food.

How Much?

In the first week, offer solid food to your baby no more than once or twice a day. Start small, 1 or 2 teaspoons in total. Your little one might not even finish that, which is totally OK. Remember, your baby is still getting lots of nutrition from breast milk or formula during this transition period. According to the AAP, infants from age 6 to 12 months need about 50 calories per pound, for a total of about 850 calories a day. By 8 months old, your baby should be consuming approximately half a cup of vegetables and half a cup of fruit per day.[33] Remember, this is just the beginning, so don't worry!

Organic or Not?

Generally, yes, organic matters—but with a few asterisks.

Currently there's not a strong body of literature supporting vast nutritional differences between organic and conventional foods. Growers do produce organic foods with fewer chemicals and in more sustainable ways. To meet USDA standards, organic crops must grow without use of pesticides, GMOs, synthetic fertilizers, irradiation, or sewage sludge. Organic livestock must eat organic food and cannot receive antibiotics or growth hormones. Pesticides, such as persistent organic pollutants (POPs), raise particular concern because their resistance to degradation means they can accumulate in our bodies. Studies show that long-term exposure to POPs can prove detrimental to humans, leading to the development of cancer, neurological problems, and endocrine system disruption.[34]

Most studies over the past few decades have shown that organic and nonorganic foods have roughly comparable nutrient content, but others concluded that certain organic foods may have higher levels of antioxidants and polyphenols, which are important for a newborn's immune system. Reviews of multiple studies show that some organic foods contain higher levels of vitamin C, iron, magnesium, and phosphorus compared to nonorganic varieties of the same foods. Likewise, strictly organic dairy products may contain more omega-3 fatty acids, necessary for cell membrane formation, which enables growth.[35] Some foods, such as peaches, strawberries, blueberries, peppers, potatoes, and spinach, consistently have high levels of chemical residues.[36]

A study conducted in the Netherlands looked at the effects of conventional versus organic foods on the development of eczema, wheezing, and other atopic manifestations within the first 2 years of life. After observing 815 infants, researchers drew an association between consuming strictly organic dairy products and a decreased risk of infant eczema. If your baby is prone to allergies, switching to organics may help alleviate atopic conditions.[37]

But organic food costs more, and not everyone can afford it. If you can't, that's OK. You still have plenty of good options for feeding your little one. Consider purchasing a mix of organic and non-organic foods. Focus your organic list on foods that consistently test high for chemical residues, as listed above.

Heavy Metals

Eating organic and cooking at home are great, but—surprise!—neither action will help you avoid heavy metals in what you eat. Trace amounts exist in the water and air, but the heavy metals we consume mostly come from soil, including the soil from organic farms. Other potential sources include artificial additives and manufacturing processes. Let's look at how worried you need to be as well as steps you can take to mitigate them.

Metals, you may recall from the periodic table, are shiny, usually malleable elements that conduct electricity and heat fairly well. Heavy metals (not to be confused with hard rock or punk) have high densities and toxicity levels. Arsenic, cadmium, lead, and mercury most commonly make their way into food products. A 2021 congressional report warned consumers of these and other toxins present in

many popular food brands for babies and toddlers. The report found that "commercial baby foods are tainted with significant levels of toxic heavy metals, including arsenic, lead, cadmium, and mercury." It also called for sweeping reforms, including phasing out certain ingredients, such as rice, in baby food products; regular testing of ingredients and final products; and the establishment of federal limits for heavy metals in baby food.[38]

Scientific evidence indicates that babies are especially vulnerable. Regular exposure, even at moderate levels, can impact neurological development because babies are smaller and developing. The major heavy metals don't have the same impact on an adult, who is 6 to 10 times bigger and has a fully formed brain. Infant exposure correlates to future IQ loss, attention-deficit issues, and behavioral problems. According to a Healthy Babies Bright Futures study, unsafe levels of heavy metals in baby food cause a loss of 11 million IQ points for children age 2 and younger.[39]

In the past decade, more than 20 peer-reviewed studies have shown a link between heavy metals and impaired brain function for kids.[40] According to a meta-analysis published in 2014, "the neurotoxic effects of arsenic appear to be most severe in the developing brain," compared to the other major heavy metals. The study estimated that children exposed to higher levels of arsenic may have, on average, about 6 fewer IQ points than their peers. A study on pregnant mothers in Bangladesh also showed a link between arsenic exposure during pregnancy and smaller head circumferences and femur lengths for their babies. The low daily exposures that children incur from heavy metals create "subclinical decrements in brain function" on a global scale. Scientists write that the exposures "diminish quality of life, reduce academic achievement, and disturb behaviour, with profound consequences for the welfare and productivity of entire societies."[41]

Babies can encounter heavy metals in their environment—such as lead from paint in older homes—but food, whether store-bought or home-cooked, acts as one of the most common pathways. Heavy metals get into our food in three main ways:

1. **SOIL.** Surprisingly enough, this is the most common conduit. Contaminated runoff, not pesticides, most commonly introduces heavy metals to the ground. Plants then absorb lead, arsenic, and other metals from the water in the soil. Some foods, including rice, pull heavy metals from the soil especially well.

2. **MANUFACTURING PROCESS.** Contaminated cooking water, food processing equipment (especially older machinery), overprocessing, and overheating certain foods also result in the increased presence of heavy metals.

3. **ARTIFICIAL ADDITIVES.** According to the 2021 congressional report, the use of certain artificial additives, such as a fortified vitamin mix, was linked to high levels of heavy metals in baby food products. The report recommended that companies regularly test their final products to minimize this risk.

In the brain, lead and iron compete for the same transporter. That means that, if a person ingests too much lead in food, competitive inhibition will block the body from absorbing the necessary iron. It's impossible to avoid all exposure, but you can take the following steps to reduce your baby's exposure to heavy metals.

No Rice or Fruit Juice

Eliminating rice dramatically reduces arsenic exposure. The 2021 congressional report and two other major reports recommend reducing rice in baby food, noting it as one of the most common ingredients for commercially made baby food products.[42] Rice cereal currently has a legal limit of 100 parts per billion for arsenic, but many rice-based baby foods test far higher than that. We typically consider brown rice healthier than the white variety, but brown rice usually tests higher for arsenic because the heavy metal concentrates in the bran layer, which processing removes from white rice.

Fruit juice also contains high amounts of arsenic and lead. A 2019 *Consumer Reports* investigation found arsenic, cadmium, and lead in popular fruit juices. You might feel comfortable giving juice to an older child, but don't make it a staple for your baby. Babies also shouldn't drink it because of the added sugar (more on that later). According to nutritionist Dahlia Rimmon, MS, RDN, water reinforces healthy drinking habits and is ultimately the best choice.

However, seeing as 4 billion juice boxes are thrown out each year, we know juice happens, especially as kids get older. The fact remains: no juice for tots under 12 months; but if you plan to purchase juice, the recommendation is to choose one that is pasteurized for food safety. Young kids are more susceptible to harmful bacteria than adults. You could also choose to make fresh juice at home, in which case Dahlia recommends consuming within 24 hours to mitigate the growth of bacteria. A juicer works perfectly for this—especially if you're making it in small amounts. If you're offering juice to your child, we recommend no more than 4 ounces per day, and/or diluting the juice in 50/50 parts with water to minimize the amount of sugar (yes, even natural sugars) taken in from beverages at one time.

> **Water consumption from 0 through 6 months comes from human milk or formula; for the next 6 months, it comes from human milk and complementary foods.**

Keep Eating the Rainbow

Variety matters. Whether you're buying or growing food, try to give your child a wide range of ingredients. Doing so ensures that your baby isn't consuming a source of nutrition potentially high in heavy metals, such as rice, all the time. A varied diet of real, whole foods has a wide range of benefits, including a healthier gut biome, greater exposure to more nutrients, and training baby to like veggies instead of sweets. See page 44 for our rainbow recommendations.

Binders and Blockers

Some foods help limit the absorption of heavy metals in the body. Binders attach themselves to heavy metals and assist in their removal from the digestive tract. Good examples include blueberries, tomatoes, and spirulina. Blockers, meanwhile, help stop the body's absorption of heavy metals. Specific nutrients, such as iron and calcium, work well as blockers. Vitamin C boosts the absorption of iron, so we recommend serving foods high in vitamin C, such as kiwifruit, papayas, peppers, and tomatoes, with iron-rich foods, including broccoli and beans.

BPA

In French and Spanish, this acronym means good agricultural practices, but in English it stands for bisphenol A, an industrial chemical used in plastics and resins since the 1950s. In America, manufacturers create more than 2.3 billion pounds of it annually. It goes into metal can coatings, baby bottles, and other objects. If you can't remember the technical term, just remember that it's a Bad Plastic Additive.

BPAs can prove just as damaging as heavy metals. Studies have shown that they seep from containers into the foods we eat.[43] Gestational BPA exposure adversely affects areas in the brain related to regulating behavior and emotions. Research shows that exposure during pregnancy, but not childhood, has an association with worse behavior at age 3, especially among girls.[44] If that doesn't gross you out, sip on this: the CDC found traces of BPA in nearly *all* the urine samples it collected in 2004 to gauge the prevalence of various chemicals in the human body. That's what we call a pee-diatric no-go.

Plant-Powered Baby

If you've flipped through the recipes in this book, you probably noticed that all of the core recipes are plant-based. We did this for two reasons. First, the biggest concern that parents share with us is how to make sure their children develop a real love for vegetables. Also, it's really easy to incorporate dairy, fish, or meat into the savory dishes. A lot of science supports the advantages of a plant-powered diet, and more people are joining the movement. A 2020 survey reported that more than 9.7 million Americans were following plant-based diets, up from just 290,000 in 2004.[45]

Plant-based diets have clear health benefits, such as lower risks of diabetes, high blood pressure, cancer, osteoporosis, and heart disease. Evidence from observational and interventional studies suggests that plant-based diets may promote health through the diverse ecosystem of beneficial bacteria in the gut. Observational studies have shown differences in the microbiota composition among omnivores, vegetarians, and vegans. Compared to omnivorous diets, vegan diets commonly contain more fiber and less saturated fat and protein. The current thinking holds that long-term vegetable consumption correlates with microbiome diversity and that higher fiber intake increases the prevalence of microbes associated with a healthy gut.[46]

As an added bonus, the production of meat and dairy also contributes to higher greenhouse gas emissions and climate crisis. If each person in America gave up meat and dairy products on 1 or more days per week, we would reduce carbon emissions and waste byproducts that end up in the oceans *significantly*. Even a slight shift from animal-based foods can help save the planet.

If you and your family are thinking about transitioning to a vegan diet, it's important to be intentional about what you eat and consume sufficient amounts of vitamin B_{12}—from foods such as mushrooms, nutritional yeast, and tempeh—and vitamin D (more mushrooms!).

According to guidance published by the AAP, plant-based diets can be a healthy option for children.[47] Atherosclerosis, the hardening and narrowing of the arteries, likely starts in childhood, so healthy eating at a young age can help your child in adulthood. According to the Academy of Nutrition and Dietetics, other benefits of a vegetarian diet in childhood and adolescence include greater consumption of fruits and vegetables, fewer sweets and salty snacks, and lower intake of saturated fat. Verdict? Consuming more plants early in life can establish lifelong healthy habits.

A plant-forward or plant-based diet isn't the same as going vegetarian or vegan. It doesn't mean avoiding all meat or dairy products. It means that a majority of the food comes from plant sources, such as fruits, grains, legumes, nuts, and vegetables. If your family eats a lot of animal products but you want to make changes, go gradually. Here are a few additional tips from the AAP:

- Eat smaller amounts of meat or eliminate it from 1 or 2 meals per week. Filling plant-protein options include beans, tofu, and nuts. Make a grown-up version of a meat-free dish that your child loves.
- Choose sources of healthy fats, such as avocados, nuts, olives, and seeds.

- At lunch and dinner, fill at least half your plate with vegetables in a variety of colors.
- Aim to eat leafy green vegetables at least once per day.
- Fruit is the new dessert. Make bananas, berries, mangoes, and plums part of your routine.[48]

Plant-Powered Nutrients

Dr. Manasa Mantravadi, an assistant professor of Clinical Pediatrics, at the Indiana University School of Medicine, and her family are vegetarians, so their plant-based diet includes eggs and dairy, but a vegan diet also can be healthy and complete. It just requires a little more planning. It's important to maximize calcium, iron, vitamin B_{12}, vitamin D, and zinc in a child's diet, so here are a few sources of these important nutrients:

- **CALCIUM:** beans, broccoli, kale, soy milk (fortified)
- **IRON:** bread (fortified), broccoli, cabbage, cereals, chickpeas, dried fruits, kale, kidney beans, lentils, tofu, and whole grains
- **VITAMIN B_{12}:** bread, cereals (fortified), nutritional yeast, soy milk, and supplements
- **VITAMIN D:** cereals (fortified), milk substitutes (fortified), mushrooms, and supplements
- **ZINC:** beans, cereals (fortified), hummus, nuts, potatoes, and pumpkin seeds

Talk to your pediatrician for more detailed advice on vegan diets for children.

What about Protein?

Most people think of meat when they think about protein, but plenty of plants pack a protein punch. According to the Harvard School of Public Health, plant protein is a healthier choice than animal protein.[49] But most parents don't know their child's protein needs, which look like this:

Age	Amount of Protein per Day
1–3 years	13 grams
4–8 years	19 grams
9+ years	46–52 grams

As you can see, it's probably much less than you thought for young kids.

Protein is an essential macronutrient at any age, and many foods can meet a child's protein needs. A vegetarian diet can include cheese, eggs, milk, and yogurt, all great sources of protein. In the legume group, go for chickpeas, hummus, lentils, peanut butter, soy milk, and tofu. Oatmeal and whole wheat pasta make great grain options, and even broccoli, peas, and potatoes contain some protein. Just make sure to keep an eye on the fat, salt, and sugar content of any food that you buy rather than make.

Your Baby on Sugar

Fruits naturally contain sugar but in appropriate amounts and in balance with fiber and other nutrients. Fruit juice concentrates sound healthy. Apple concentrate is just concentrated apples, right? Nope! The concentration process removes all fiber and most nutrients, leaving mostly sugars.

Overconsumption of sugar in Western diets, an increasing problem, is contributing to rising obesity levels. According to a *Washington Post* article by our friend and advisor Michael Goran, professor of preventive medicine and pediatrics at the University of Southern California, "The sugars that a mother consumes while pregnant or nursing can be passed to her baby, disrupt healthy growth and development, and pose risk for obesity."[50] One of Goran's recent studies showed that fructose, or fruit sugar, consumed by mothers was detectable in breast milk and correlated to an increased risk of obesity for their babies. As a survival mechanism, babies naturally prefer the sweetness of fruit to the bitterness of vegetables. Added sugar before age 2 is bad news, though, and can put a child at risk for developing health complications.[51]

Facts about Sugar

The brain needs some sugar to function, and the body can absorb it from a variety of foods such as breast milk and fruit. But manufacturers have developed more than 50 synonyms for added sugar. (See the next section.) America has become the world's largest per-capita consumer of sugar, and fruit-based sugars and sweeteners are becoming more prolific. Sometimes they even contain *more* sugar than high-fructose corn syrup.

Kids have a built-in preference for sweetness, but this survival mechanism is backfiring in today's high-sugar environment. Young children are consuming more sugar in liquid form—and different types of sugar that can disrupt healthy growth and development—than ever before. A child doesn't need to be overweight to have a sugar problem. Too much sugar impairs a child's ability to achieve age-appropriate tasks, such as building a tower of blocks at age 2, taking standardized tests in middle school, or writing a college application essay at age 17. Some people think that kids get a free pass to eat whatever they want and that only adults have to worry about what they eat. This pass doesn't exist and never did.

As Dr. Goran often reminds us, too much sugar literally shrinks the brain. High amounts of fructose reduce brain plasticity and long-term memory function—at any age.

Synonyms for Sugar

Some common synonyms and substitutes for sugar include agave nectar, agave syrup, barley malt, beet sugar, blackstrap molasses, brown rice syrup, brown sugar, buttercream, cane juice (evaporated), cane sugar, caramel, carob syrup, castor sugar, coconut sugar, confectioners' (powdered) sugar, corn syrup, corn syrup solids, crystalline fructose, date sugar, Demerara sugar, dextrin, dextrose, diastatic malt, ethyl maltol, Florida Crystals, fructose, fruit juice, fruit juice concentrate, galactose, glucose, glucose syrup solids, golden sugar, golden syrup, grape sugar, high-fructose corn syrup, honey, icing sugar, invert sugar, lactose, malt syrup, maltodextrin, maltose, maple syrup, molasses, muscovado sugar, panela sugar, raw sugar, refiner's syrup, rice syrup, sorghum syrup, Sucanat, sucrose, treacle, turbinado sugar, and yellow sugar.

Fruit Juice Is Not a Friend

In recent years, as guidelines around sugar have tightened, so have recommendations on juice. The AAP recently advised that children under age 1 shouldn't drink fruit juice.

For childhood constipation, use prunes puréed with water instead of apple, pear, or prune juice. Prune juice lacks fiber, so manufacturers add sorbitol, a sugar alcohol that has laxative properties. Puréed prunes offer the laxative properties of fiber and contain other beneficial nutrients that the juicing process removes. The combination of fiber and water will alleviate the constipation.

Be mindful of how much total fruit you give your kid. Because of their fiber content, whole fruits definitely outrank juice, but a diet too rich in fruits will increase fructose consumption and limit room for other nutrient-rich veggies and proteins. Maintaining a good variety will help you hit those nutrients that kids typically lack, such as iron, and will help your child develop a love for real food.

Salt and Other No-Fly Foods

The AAP says no salt before age 1. As we grow, sodium becomes a necessary nutrient, but children up to age 12 months are getting what they need from breast milk or formula. Babies need less than 1 gram of salt per day. Their tiny kidneys can't process much more than that. Also be mindful of your kid's salt intake. Finger foods and family foods usually contain more than enough sodium. Use salt sporadically and in limited amounts while cooking.

Until 12 months, your baby also should avoid:

- Honey (even baked), which can contain bacteria that can cause infant botulism
- Too much cow's milk, which can lead to anemia and nutrient loss from not eating other foods
- Soda and bottled iced tea, which usually contain too much sugar and caffeine
- Yogurt drinks and fruit blends, which typically contain loads of added sugar
- Processed foods for adults, such as canned vegetables, which can contain a lot of preservatives, artificial colors, flavors, and other chemicals

Next let's dig into how taste preferences form and how we can help our kiddos by exposing them to varied flavor profiles early and often.

Flavor & Culture

FUTURE FOODIES START HERE

CHEAT SHEET

In this chapter, we dive headfirst into where food and society
intersect, including:
- The importance of taste buds
- Your role as a food model
- How to avoid creating a picky eater
- A checklist for starting solids
- Whether baby-led weaning is worth it

You've heard the word "gestation," but what about *gustation*?
That's the medical word for the sense of taste. It's important to
everyone but especially your little one. In the early days, while
other senses and motor skills remain less developed, it directly
affects nutritional impact.

As we've seen, babies experience flavors during gestation. If you eat a lot of garlic, your baby will develop a taste for it. Unlike crawling, talking, walking, flushing a toilet, and other learned abilities, your baby can taste from birth. As with touch and smell, there's less of a learning curve with tasting than with other motor skills. Taste ability changes slightly during infancy, but it's still highly malleable. The function itself doesn't change much, but the preferences associated with it can and do change dramatically.

Infants don't have an innate curiosity for new foods, but multiple studies point to this period, from weaning to about 3 years old, as the most crucial time for future food acceptance. During this window, children's "perception, cognition, behaviors, and experiences" are incredibly sensitive when it comes to eating. Between ages 3 and 4, a child's basic taste palate has formed, so everything your child eats before that stretch determines the foundation.[1]

First Tastes

We humans have been refining our taste buds since our earliest days.

> Taste helps us decide what to eat and influences how efficiently we digest these foods. Human taste abilities have been shaped, in large part, by the ecological niches our evolutionary ancestors occupied and by the nutrients they sought. Early hominids sought nutrition within a closed tropical forest environment, probably eating mostly fruit and leaves, and early hominids left this environment for the savannah and greatly expanded their dietary repertoire. They would have used their sense of taste to identify nutritious food items. The risks of making poor food selections when foraging not only entail wasted energy and metabolic harm from eating foods of low nutrient and energy content, but also the harmful and potentially lethal ingestion of toxins. The learned consequences of ingested foods may subsequently guide our future food choices.[2]

That makes sense in terms of evolution, but as we mentioned in Chapter 2, the flavors that babies experience in utero can influence food acceptance at weaning. Have you ever heard that babies don't have taste buds? That's a myth!

Fiction	Fact
Babies don't have taste buds.	**A baby's taste buds start forming in utero.**

Let's say it again: flavor exposure begins in the womb. By weeks 13 to 15 of pregnancy, a baby's first taste buds appear. (Teeny, tiny, baby taste buds—so cute!) Craving curry? If you scarf a bowl of that zesty goodness, your baby will sense those spices through the amniotic fluid. But that's just the beginning of the equation.

Your Role as a Food Model

As we saw at the beginning of Chapter 2, your role as a parent matters because you matter—in lots of different ways. One of the most important is that you have agency in your child's relationship with food.

That relationship starts in utero and continues through childhood. Research shows, for example, that alcohol consumed by a lactating woman transfers to her milk. About 2 percent of consumed booze reaches the boob.[3] That might not sound like a big deal but think about how small your little one is. Then consider that alcohol affects sleep, motor development, and even early reactions to alcohol.[4] One study found that infants with "more exposure to alcohol behaved differently in the presence of an alcohol-scented toy than did infants with less alcohol exposure. Specifically, infants who had more exposure to alcohol demonstrated more mouthing of the alcohol-scented toy, but not of the other toys, than did infants with less alcohol exposure."[5]

Exposure matters as a negative but even more so as a positive. While breastfeeding, an infant can experience multiple flavors. You need to train your baby's palate so your little one develops healthful food preferences. Lots of studies show that early exposure to a wide variety of textures and flavors can reduce fussiness and instill a love of healthy foods later in life. In a 2013 study conducted across three countries in Europe, researchers found that "increasing variety and frequency of vegetable offering between 6 and 12 months, when children are most receptive, may promote vegetable consumption in children."

A 2021 study from Finland hypothesized that mothers' food preferences had a greater influence on children's fruit and vegetable preferences than their fathers'. Moms who liked veggies had kids who liked veggies, the study found, but it also concluded that dads had a positive influence on preferences for strong-tasting vegetables and berries as well.[6] That tells us that the entire household has an effect on eating preferences.

An Australian study aimed to identify key characteristics of a home environment associated with higher consumption of fruits and vegetables. Parents reported the variety and frequency of those foods that their preschool children consumed, and researchers found positive associations between parental intake and children's intake, availability and accessibility, the number of occasions that parents provided their children with fruit and vegetables, and allowing children to eat only at set mealtimes all or most of the time. Combined, these aspects of the home food environment accounted for 48 percent of a child's fruit and vegetable score.[7]

Your own eating attitude, what researchers call your food "competence," contributes to your child's eating attitude. Mothers who consume more vegetables also tend to reoffer vegetables more frequently. Other studies show that parents even use different strategies for fruits compared to vegetables. We tend to approach fruit with a more positive vibe but veggies more negatively.[8] We also give in too easily. When it comes to reoffering vegetables—meaning the 12 to 15 times it can take a child to accept a new food—a UK study found mothers "significantly less likely to reoffer rejected vegetables if they were concerned about time, money, and waste, were influenced by their child's mood, or were concerned about their child having tantrums."[9] Which of course makes human sense. It's hard to live by the old saw, "If at first you don't succeed, try, try again," when dealing with a tantrum and wasted food.

It's not easy, but try to be patient. Your future foodie will thank you. Overexposure to sweetened foods during this period will encourage kids to develop a preference for sugars, so you've got to try, try again.

Social Feeding

We all do it: scroll, scroll, scroll. Look up. *Everything OK? Yep, looks good*. Scroll, scroll. Or we react negatively to something frustrating, which quickly imprints on a young, developing mind. The social aspect of getting your baby to like new foods plays a huge part in the process. When it comes to socialization and feeding practices, keep the following points in mind.

Bonding starts on day 1. Nursing or bottle-feeding is a bonding activity. Providing any kind of delicious, nutritious food strengthens that bond. Babies look to caregivers for cues that they show interest and care. Eating healthy is no exception.

It doesn't have to be a formal, sit-down, 5-course meal, either. Family-style meals promote responsive feeding and provide the same nutrition as plated meals.[10]

Mealtime is shared time. Always try to sit with and engage your little one while eating. By sitting together, you'll help baby learn safe and appropriate eating behaviors. You also will model eating as an enjoyable activity beyond just the food. From 12 to 24 months, babies naturally focus on mimicking and pleasing behaviors. Demonstrate a good attitude. Many studies confirm caregivers' roles in shaping children's eating habits. Observation and imitation of behaviors and reactions of surrounding people shape their attitudes toward food. While your baby is eating, your face will affect if and how the little one tries a novel food. One study showed that children were much more likely to try an unknown food when their mothers simultaneously chowed down and reacted enthusiastically. This reaction was even stronger than when the parent only verbally encouraged the child to try the food.[11]

As your baby enters the dreaded picky-eater phase, forcing the kiddo to eat seems like an obvious solution. But punishment for refusing to eat can result in increased reluctance to eat. Many studies have confirmed that the more authoritatively parents behave toward children during meals, the more often children reject the food. One study in particular found that the difficulty of feeding children 20 to 36 months resulted mainly from parents' authoritarian practices by which they force children to consume rejected food.[12] We know it's hard but try to keep your cool and stay positive. Remember, you're the adult! Blowing your lid can prolong neophobic behavior—more about that shortly—which is a lose-lose.

Picky Eating

As a parent, you have to accept some hard truths. One of them is that picky eaters are made, not born. Scientists have identified genetic variants that code for taste receptors less receptive to bitter flavors or more receptive to sweet flavors.[13] So nature is part of the equation, but the rest is nurture—specifically what you as a parent put on the menu. Guess what the most popular vegetable for toddlers in America is. Carrots? You might think so, but no. It's the french fry.[14] Children in the depths of the Amazonian rain forest, for example, aren't wondering, *Where's my Happy Meal?* They're eating from a different menu. We have way more options than fries, but that means you have to come to terms with your agency in this process. Lots of kids love broccoli, kale, and spinach without making *grosssss* faces. Even babies can learn to love veggies. When it comes to food, you, as a parent, have an active role in your child's acceptance or fussiness.

Fiction	Fact
I just have a picky eater.	**Repeated exposure to novel flavors during breastfeeding and complementary feeding increases a child's willingness to try new foods within a positive social environment.**

Let's take a look at some of the challenges and then at some of the strategies to surmount them.

Sugar Shock

Grocery shelves teem with highly processed, non-nutritious, shelf-stable baby purée options. Many are, in a word, *gross*. Manufacturers process it at high temperatures for long periods of time to achieve shelf stability of 1 to 2 years. Look more closely at most products in the baby food aisle, and you'll often find additives, fortifications, preservatives, high-fructose ingredients, and sometimes straight-up sugar. Angela and Evelyn founded Yumi in large part because of all of the fructose in the baby food aisle.

So. Much. Sugar.

For survival, our brains biologically prefer caloric, mineral-rich foods that taste sweet or salty, while rejecting anything potentially toxic that tastes bitter or sour. That dichotomy causes problems. According to the CDC, the American adult obesity rate currently sits at 42.4 percent, and that rate has increased by 26 percent since 2008. The coronavirus pandemic exacerbated these numbers, especially among children. Obesity now affects 1 in 5 children and adolescents in the country, a number that has tripled since the 1970s.[15] Childhood obesity has reached epidemic levels, and food is the top culprit. We even know where and when it began.

In 1916, fry cook Walter Anderson borrowed $80 to open his first hamburger stand. After opening four more, he partnered with real estate and insurance agent Billy Ingram to build the first stand under the name of White Castle, which launched in Wichita, Kansas, in March 1921. Now operating in more than 400 locations (although not in Kansas anymore, Toto), White Castle often receives credit as the first fast-food joint. Before Anderson's burgers, the ability to make food "fast" didn't exist yet. White Castle changed the way we eat and even the dynamics of the home. It also helped create the food-industrial complex. Add the processed foods that hit the scene in the 1920s, and you have a chef's-kiss recipe for diet disaster.

Today, ultra-processed foods are everywhere, and they contain little to no whole food. Almost 60 percent of calories consumed in America between 2007 and 2012 came from processed foods.[16] This data is troubling for a number of reasons. Those foods likely triggered the rise in obesity and chronic diseases in the past decades. Ultra-processed foods serve as the major dietary vector for added sugars. An increase in ultra-processed foods means a decrease in protein; fiber; calcium; magnesium; phosphorus; potassium; vitamins A, C, D, and E; and zinc; and an increase of simple carbohydrates and saturated fat.[17]

As the eating public wises up to the dangers of these ultra-processed time bombs, the food industry simultaneously gets better at hiding harmful ingredients. Our food isn't addictive in the way we think. We're addicted to highly engineered additives that make "food" taste "delicious." We're addicted to chemicals. That bag of chips you can't stop eating? Natural selection has predisposed you to crave foods high in sugar and fat. While writing this paragraph, Arianna polished off an afternoon bowl of Honey Nut Cheerios, and Evelyn took down a bowl of ice cream for lunch. Cheerios, despite what we want to believe, aren't much better than ramen. Add a little salt and you've got lunch. Cornmeal, soy meal, hydrogenated oils, and wheat rule the center aisles of grocery stores. That's why nutritionists advise you to "shop the perimeter."

Baby food on store shelves is often older than your baby.

More problematic than our survivalist desires, foods that once contained no sweeteners now often feature high-fructose corn syrup and its awful friends—just to make them more addictive. Take pasta sauce, for example. Most pasta sauces on shelves include added sugar to sweeten the pot. What's one food that virtually all kids will eat? You got it: pas-ketti. Flip back to page 60 for a refresher on the food industry's sneaky names for sugar. An ingredient by any other name undoubtedly tastes as sweet. You don't have time to check the back of everything you buy for every item on that list, making it nearly impossible to know what you don't know.

Cookie-Crunching the Numbers

Many cereals marketed to children contain *more* sugar per serving than cookies. A 2014 Environmental Working Group study evaluated more than 1,500 cereals, 180 of them targeted to children. The EWG reported that "A child eating one serving per day of a children's cereal containing the average amount of sugar would consume nearly 1,000 teaspoons of sugar in a year."[18] That doesn't include any other meal, snack, or juice. Most cereals don't make for a nutritious breakfast, yet a 2017 survey of 1,000 parents reported troubling results, including that:

- 95 percent of children eat cereal for breakfast on school days.
- 71 percent of children drink fruit juice for breakfast on school days.
- 23 percent of kids who eat breakfast on the go drink regular or diet soda with breakfast.[19]

Keep your eyes peeled for added sugars and look at the total amount of sugar in your kid's food. Choose brands that cap the sugar content. By voting with your wallet, you'll pressure the industry to make healthier decisions. But, yes, we recognize that the system stinks and that we all sacrifice nutrition on the altar of convenience. With so many sugars hiding in plain sight and our biology working against us, we have to fight a war on multiple fronts. Throw in the sleep deprivation of a new parent who doesn't have the time or energy to read every nutrition label, and we've got kids bingeing sugar from day 1.

Future Foodies Start Here

Some children have more refined palates than adults. Kwame Onwuachi doesn't have children, but the James Beard Award–winning chef created two exclusive blends for Yumi in 2020. His Carrot and Peas Combo and a Butternut Squash Curry Blend both took inspiration from a braised oxtail dish. Raised by a chef mother who exposed him to a variety of flavors in his youth, Onwuachi believes that introducing children to many foods and spices creates healthy eaters for life. He calls food "culture on a plate," and he knows that variety matters when it comes to developing an award-winning palate.

Babies love new experiences. We all are born ready to learn. Food forms part of that learning process, and a baby's openness to new flavors reaches its highest point in infants up to age 12 months. Then it decreases with age. Your baby's reluctance or even refusal to eat certain foods results from late introduction of new foods into your kiddo's diet.

But with a blank palate, you have a great opportunity to train those taste buds. For new parents just trying to make it through the day, taste training can prove difficult. Studies show that it takes between 12 and 15 exposures for a child to accept a new food. Negative reactions—you know, screaming, crying, yelling, throwing food, refusing to eat—cause many parents to give up. If possible, don't start eliminating too many foods too early. Also try not to project your own preferences. Beets have one of the most polarizing flavors. Some people love their earthiness. Others hate them on a visceral level. But as a parent, you need to focus on variety, not just your faves.

Introducing new foods to your baby probably will result in some funny faces. This is a natural reaction to the new sensations that eating brings. If you offer the food and your child opens his or her mouth, that's a sign for more. Yay! If you get a clear refusal, give that food a rest and try again in a couple of days. If you can manage it, keep track of which foods you introduced when on a notepad or your phone. That will help you space apart refused foods and make sure you get to the 12 necessary exposures. If baby still doesn't like something, you have proof that you tried! The goal is to expose your child to a wide variety of flavors and textures and to repeat these exposures many times during ages 6 to 12 months.

Veggies early and veggies often, as hard as it may seem. You need to do it now because, from ages 2 to 5 (and let's not even think about the finicky teenage years), children become particularly neophobic about food. That's where it can get really tricky.

Neophobia

Children reject fruits and vegetables most often.[20] But are we trapped in this matrix of rejection, or can we break free? Two main factors contribute to the rejection of fruits, veggies, and unknown foods: picky eating and neophobia, a fancy Greek word for the fear of something new that has nothing to do with Keanu Reeves (shoutout to our older millennial parents).

Picky eaters might accept new foods, but they consume inadequate variety. They reject familiar *and* unfamiliar foods. Thankfully this behavior proves temporary, appearing most commonly between ages 2 and 3. It will come as a shock to exactly zero parents that, during this toddler phase, children seek new ways to assert their authority. Want them to eat veggies? NO! Did they love bananas yesterday? YES! Do they want them today? NO! Picky eaters limit their range of food but often consume larger amounts of acceptable items than their neophobic counterparts.

With food, neophobia manifests as a continued reluctance to eat new fare. In terms of evolution, neophobic behavior had an important function. Avoiding unknown foods helped protect us from eating something poisonous. It kept us alive. Now it makes parents want to pull their hair out. Studies show that children with high levels of neophobia reject food based on initial stimuli: sight, smell, and occasionally touch. Children who exhibit neophobic behavior show less inclination even to taste certain foods. Negative experiences with new foods also make matters worse. Mealtime with fussy children quickly can become a source of stress and anxiety for parent and child that negatively affects the little one's eating behavior.[21]

It can feel like a pressure cooker situation. The crankiness of hunger and exhaustion, personality factors, and feeding styles all exacerbate the situation and increase the magnitude and duration of these challenging behaviors. So what's a parent to do?

Keep reading.

The Baby-Likes-It Checklist for Starting Solids

You don't want your baby to hate veggies and eat junk. There's no anti-broccoli revolution for holdouts to join. No one we know of (aside from President George H. W. Bush) has ever gotten in a dustup over a crop of cruciferous foods. We all want the best for our babies. Keep these points in mind as you start solids.

- Genetics determine sensitivity to bitterness, and intensity depends on the number of taste buds on the tongue.

- Children's brains are developing, so they experience taste differently than adults.

- Babies make funny faces when encountering new flavors. They prefer what they know and like. But babies need variety, and they need nutrition from increasingly varied solids as they grow.

- As studies show, the more days that babies are exposed to a food, the more likely their facial expressions will change, suggesting they like it.

- Studies also show that, when vegetables are given alone, it takes longer for babies' facial expressions to indicate that they like the food—because why would they make this easy on us?

- Food exposure separated by 2 or 3 days gives you enough time to spot an allergy but not enough time for kiddos to establish liking a food.

- Eight to 10 days of repetition will give you the best chance of creating a strong food preference, especially for vegetables.

- Persistence with new foods will foster good habits early and meet less resistance later.

- Chasers help. One study found that repeated exposure to green beans and peaches increased intake, but only the babies who ate the peaches after the green beans appeared to like the taste of the green beans more after 8 days of exposure. By chasing the vegetable with the sweet, baby associates the vegetable with tasting good. Eventually you can phase out the sweet.

- You want your little one to *like* the food, not just eat it. For babies resistant to vegetables, alternating with sweet bites or using vegetable-fruit blends encourages vegetable consumption and future affinity.

- When babies open wide, stick out their tongues, and don't grimace or shudder, those are signs of liking the food.

Baby-Led Weaning

Now the million-dollar question about a hot topic: baby-led weaning or, as one dad called it: "baby linguine."

The first handful of months looks fairly simple when it comes to food. Then, around 6 months, babies start exhibiting signs that they're ready for solids. See page 50 for a refresher on those signs. Many parents start with single-ingredient purées and, during the course of a few months, introduce more textured and combined flavors. Baby-led weaning, or the Rapley Method, skips the purées and spoons entirely.

Gill Rapley coined the term for this technique in her book *Baby-Led Weaning*. Also described as "self-feeding," the practice introduces babies to solid foods by allowing them to feed themselves: no spoons, hand to face, food all over the floor. It starts at 6 months and emphasizes discovery and enjoyment. Baby sits with the family at mealtime and makes a mess!

Messes aside, many parents praise the Rapley Method as a fuss-free way to introduce food to babies ready for solids. It allows babies to explore color, smell, texture, and taste on their own and at their own pace. It encourages confidence and independence, helps with hand-eye coordination, develops chewing skills, and may make picky eating and mealtime battles less likely to occur. According to devotees, all babies can start feeding themselves around 6 months old. They just need the opportunity. The most common concern centers on choking. Never leave your baby alone or unattended with any food.

We don't think parents have to choose just one path, though. Baby-led weaning can foster independent, adventurous eaters, but a lot of that nutrition also ends up on the floor. We generally recommend a dual approach to our parents. Purées maximize the nutrition getting into your baby's belly, but baby-led weaning can help form good eating habits. Nutritious food is nutritious food, whether in smoothie form or something more gnawable. Too much parenting advice makes you feel like you have to pick a side and vehemently judge anyone who takes a different path. We're always anti shame and pro letting science and your intuition lead.

Deciding whether baby-led weaning is right for your family is a personal choice. If it sounds good to you, give it a go and see what happens. Talk to your pediatrician if you have questions. If the chaos causes more stress than structured feeding, skip it—or do a little of column A and a little of column B. Your comfort as a parent is paramount because your baby will read your cues. Happy parent, happy mealtime.

Building Blocks

WHAT ARE YOU MADE OF?

CHEAT SHEET

In this chapter, we look at the key nutrients needed in utero and during the first 2 years. We dive deeper into topics discussed in Chapter 2 and provide a full breakdown of minerals and vitamins, looking at:
- Macronutrients, micronutrients, and what they do
- Which nutrients your little one needs in what amounts
- How select nutrients interact in the human body
- The foods and tools you should have in your kitchen

Science still doesn't understand a lot about them, but our bodies do a pretty miraculous job of taking care of us—even when we don't treat them as temples. Chances are you've eaten a lot of junk in your life. Our imperfectability makes us human, and the 60 chemical elements inside your body make you function.

Of these 60, the FDA has identified 12 key minerals that we need daily. Calcium, chloride, copper, iodine, iron, magnesium, manganese, molybdenum, phosphorus, potassium, selenium, and zinc all help build healthy bones, carry red blood cells, and support brain function. In America, most nutrient deficiencies don't arise from poverty or disease. They develop because too many parents don't understand the importance of those nutrients. We eat high-calorie diets with low nutrient density. When you think about why, it's not that surprising. Big Food and Madison Avenue have focused on fat and the impact of calories on our waistlines. Few companies care whether you're getting enough folate today.

A few sobering statistics:

- More than half of Americans have low levels of vitamin D.

- More than half of American kids don't get enough vitamin D or E.

- Up to a third of American children under age 2 consume no fruits or veggies on any given day.[1] None, zero, zilch.

- Globally, about 40 percent of kids under age 5 are anemic.[2]

- More than a quarter of children don't consume enough calcium, magnesium, or vitamin A.

Many parents don't realize that their children lack a particular nutrient because those insufficiencies often have no obvious signs. Pediatricians don't test for deficiencies unless a specific concern arises. Newborns, of course, are particularly vulnerable to this problem.[3] Unfortunately, there's no way to make up for it later. You can't have a vitamin cram session.

Nutrient deficiencies are associated with weakened immune systems, stunted growth, obesity, reduced mental ability, chronic diseases, and even tooth decay. Yep, a bad diet can cause bad teeth. Malnutrition can result in reduced skull size, which can lead to metal mouth because malnourishment changes the spatial arrangement of teeth in the jaw.[4]

But you're not reading this book for strategies to avoid orthodontia. You want to know what to feed your baby for breakfast. Well, get ready because we're going to break it down slowly, starting with macronutrients and micronutrients.

First, a quick biology lesson. Roughly 96 percent of the human body consists of just four elements: oxygen, carbon, hydrogen, and nitrogen, most of that in the form of water. The remaining 4 percent sparsely samples the greatest hits of the periodic table. As a group, macronutrients encompass carbohydrates, protein, and fat. Micronutrients, as a group, entail minerals and vitamins. We need more macronutrients, but micronutrients ensure that our bodies function properly. Our bodies don't produce most vitamins that we need, so we obtain them from food or the environment.

Let's break down, step by step, what children and pregnant women need and when.[5]

Macronutrients

These are the big-picture, big-ticket categories of what we need from our food.

Carbohydrates

Carbohydrates provide energy.[6] They help the brain, central nervous system, kidneys, metabolism, and muscles function.[7] In short, they make people go zoom, including wee ones. You can find them mostly in starchy foods, such as fruits, grains, milk, and potatoes. Beans, nuts, and seeds also contain carbs.

Depending on their chemical structure, carbs fall into one of two categories: simple or complex. Simple-carbohydrate sources, which have shorter chains of molecules, include fruits (fructose) and milk products (galactose). Simple carbs include many added sugars that are usually refined and stripped of their natural fiber and nutrients, and often feature in candy, soda, syrup, and table sugar. Complex carbs, which take longer to digest, are typically better for you and associated with more whole foods and more vitamins and minerals. Simple carbs, on the other hand, are often associated with food products with low nutritional value.

Infants under 6 months need roughly 1½ grams of carbohydrates per kilogram of body weight per day; from 7 to 12 months, 1.1 grams per kilogram per day; and kids 1 to 3 years old usually get roughly 130 grams per day.[8] In the first 4 to 6 months of life, breastfeeding remains the best diet. Breast milk contains lots of good carbs and helps develop your little one's microflora (good gut bacteria). If boobing it isn't in the cards for you, all infant formula in the United States contains carbohydrate sources to mimic the composition of breast milk, and your baby will break down those carbs for energy. The most common form is lactose, which studies have shown helps gut microbiota.[9] Boob or bottle, your baby is set.

Simple Carbs

We call sugars simple because their molecular structure allows for quick and easy absorption—*too* easily and *too* quickly. Too much sugar isn't good for us, but why? . . . especially when evolution has predisposed us to like it, and it tastes so good!

The main problem lies in concentration. In nature, sugars exist in small amounts alongside larger volumes of water, fiber, and other nutrients. In many forms of simple carbs, food producers remove them from their plant sources and refine, process, and condense them. In that ratio, they cause a reaction in the body more like a drug than food. Sugar triggers the release of opioids and dopamine, and studies have shown that, at the neurobiological level, a sugar high feels more intense than cocaine. Drugs such as cocaine activate the same pathways in the brain that respond to sweet rewards.[10] Eaten in large amounts, concentrated sugars cause a dramatic rise in blood sugar levels, which throws the pancreas and other digestive organs into overdrive. That overreaction causes an equally swift drop in blood sugar levels. That sugar crash affects your brain before any other organ: you feel tired, irritable, nervous, and light-headed, and you may experience other low blood sugar (hypoglycemia) symptoms.

Many simple carbs supply empty calories, meaning they contain few vitamins or minerals. Consuming them in large amounts makes you feel full for a short time, but you burn them quickly and soon feel hungry again. They deplete you of vitamins and minerals already in your body, leaving you in nutritional debt.

Products labeled "all natural" can contain loads of sugar because many forms of sugar are also 100 percent natural. Any words in an ingredient list that end in -ose are sugars. Food manufacturers sometimes break sugar into multiple -oses. A jar labeled "pear, dextrose, sucrose, and fructose" probably has more sugar in it than pear once you add together all of those -oses. Keep this equation in mind when you look at a label: 4.2 grams of sugar = 1 teaspoon. A typical 12-ounce soft drink contains about 9 teaspoons of sugar.

Complex Carbs

Carbohydrates with more intricate molecular structures take hours to be digested. The process releases them into the bloodstream slowly and steadily. Blood sugar levels stay at an even keel, along with organ activity and your emotions. After eating complex carbs, you won't feel hungry again for several hours. They feature in grains, legumes, nuts, seeds, and potatoes.

Fiber, a particularly healthy type of complex carb, comes only from plants. There's no fiber in meat, eggs, milk, or cheese (sigh). You can find it in whole grains, legumes, nuts, seeds, pectin, cellulose, guar gum, and in parts of fruits and vegetables, particularly the peels but also the stringy membranes between orange segments and celery strings. Yum!

Ever see guar gum in an ingredient list and wonder, *What's that?* **It sounds a little menacing, but it's just a whitish powder made from guar beans, also called cluster beans, that stabilizes and thickens certain foods.**

Fiber also falls into two categories: insoluble and soluble. Insoluble fiber, including lignin, cellulose, and hemicellulose, doesn't dissolve in water and adds bulk to the diet. It speeds the passage of food through the intestine, which helps prevent constipation, and speeds carcinogens out of the body before they can do much harm, thereby helping to reduce cancer risk. Soluble fiber, such as pectin, gums, and psyllium, also increases bulk in the diet but dissolves in water. It slows the absorption of carbs, which helps manage blood sugar levels and can lower blood cholesterol levels.

Lignin, a fiber ingredient and woody material from plant stems and bark, is great for making paper but not so much for dinner.

Good food sources of insoluble fiber include legumes (beans, lentils, peas, soy), oats, barley, apples, pears, plums, and citrus. Good sources of soluble fiber include whole grains (bread, cereal, crackers, muffins, pasta, rolls, etc.), vegetables, and fruits with peels, nuts, and seeds.

Recommended Daily Intake of Carbohydrates
- Pregnant and lactating mothers: 175 grams
- 0–6 months: 60 grams
- 7–12 months: 95 grams
- 1–2 years: 130 grams

Good food sources include: corn, legumes, peas, potatoes, starchy vegetables, whole-grain breads.

Protein

The body needs a regular supply of protein to make, repair, and replace its parts. Your body replaces fat cells within a year, and no blood cell inside you is more than 4 months old, which is pretty cute because blood cells are such fast learners. It strengthens bones, muscles, the circulatory system, hormone function, cartilage, and skin. It does all of that by providing information and energy—like a USB cable—but your body has to break it down into amino acids first. The body stores fat and carbohydrates, but it doesn't store protein. Vegans can meet all of the body's protein needs with vegetables and fruits.

> **Bran is a good source of fiber, but too much of it can strip important nutrients from the body.**

It's difficult to establish recommended protein intake for children because requirements from birth to 6 months fall in with total energy requirements. But proportionate to size, babies need more protein than adults because they're growing at a rapid rate, from brains to muscles, and adding new cells each day, along with all of that repairing and replacing. An adult needs about a third of a gram of protein for each pound of body weight, but a baby needs approximately a full gram for each pound of body weight, or three times the adult amount.

Recommended Daily Intake of Protein
- Pregnant and lactating mothers: 71 grams
- 6–12 months: 11 grams (from breast milk or formula)
- 1–3 years old: 13 grams

Good food sources include: dairy, eggs, guava, legumes, poultry.

Fat

Historically, it's gotten a bad rap—but thanks to science and increased education, the tide is turning and more people are becoming aware of how absolutely essential fat is. It ensures normal growth and development (especially for brains!), cushions organs, and provides energy. We often misstep while considering how much fat our bodies need, though. As with carbs, consumption of excess fat can lead to obesity because the body stores unutilized fat. Elevated levels of saturated and trans fats can lead to cardiovascular disease or cancer.

For children younger than age 2, fats represent a crucial element of their diet. Toddlers have small stomachs, which can take only limited amounts of food at a time. Dietary fat helps provide the energy they need to grow. It also helps develop the brain and assists in wound healing. Insufficient fat intake correlates with smaller brains, fewer neurons, and simpler synaptic architecture.[11]

Recommended Daily Intake of Fat
- Pregnant and lactating mothers: 65 grams
- 0–6 months: 31 grams
- 7–12 months: 30 grams
- 1–2 years: not yet determined (limited data)

Good food sources include: avocados, chocolate, coconut, dairy, fish, nuts, olives, poultry, seeds, soy.

Micronutrients

At a more granular level, these essential elements and compounds also ensure proper functioning and well-being. This section takes a closer look at 16 minerals: calcium, chloride, chromium, copper, fluoride, iodine, iron, magnesium, manganese, molybdenum, phosphorus, potassium, selenium, sodium, sulfur, and zinc; as well as 14 vitamins: biotin, choline, folic acid, and vitamins A, B_1, B_2, B_3, B_5, B_6, B_{12}, C, D, E, and K.

Minerals

These stars of the periodic table of elements—excluding carbon, hydrogen, nitrogen, and oxygen because of their ubiquity and accessibility—enable life as we know it.

Calcium

You and baby need calcium for strong bones, muscles, and teeth, and for proper blood clotting. During pregnancy, it decreases blood pressure and prevents leg cramps. Abnormally low calcium levels occur more frequently in newborns, especially preemies. Deficiency can lead to osteoporosis, rickets, and stunting. Calcium limits the absorption of iron, so don't supplement those two minerals simultaneously.

Recommended Daily Intake of Calcium
- Pregnant and lactating mothers: 1,300 milligrams
- 0–6 months: 200 milligrams

- 7–12 months: 260 milligrams
- 1–3 years: 700 milligrams

Good food sources include: almonds, dairy, soy, winter squash.

Chloride

One of the most important electrolytes in the bloodstream, chloride powers the production of stomach acid, which breaks down proteins and fights bacteria. Chlorine deficiency is rare, seeing that most foods that contain sodium also provide chloride. You might recall that sodium chloride = salt. Remember, do not add salt for infants younger than age 1.

Recommended Daily Intake of Chloride
- Pregnant and lactating mothers: 2,300 milligrams
- 0–6 months: 180 milligrams
- 7–12 months: 570 milligrams
- 1–3 years: 1,500 milligrams

Good food sources include: celery, lettuce, olives, rye, seaweed, tomatoes.

Chromium

This antioxidant—meaning that it prevents damage caused by free radicals—helps regulate blood sugar, lowers bad cholesterol (LDL), and raises good cholesterol (HDL). Up to 90 percent of Americans have low levels of chromium, leading to raised blood sugar and triglycerides, thereby increasing the risk of heart disease, but severe deficiency is rare. For babies, especially those at risk for hyperglycemia (high blood sugar), chromium helps with glucose tolerance.[12]

Recommended Daily Intake of Chromium
- Pregnant mothers: 30 micrograms
- Lactating mothers: 45 micrograms
- 0–6 months: 0.2 microgram
- 7–12 months: 5.5 micrograms
- 1–3 years: 11 micrograms

Good food sources include: apples, broccoli, green beans, nutritional yeast, potatoes, seafood, whole grains.

Copper

When partnered with iron, copper helps form red blood cells. Deficiency can cause impaired growth, bone abnormalities, anemia, and reduced white blood cell count.

Recommended Daily Intake of Copper
- Pregnant mothers: 1,000 micrograms
- Lactating mothers: 1,300 micrograms
- 0–6 months: 200 micrograms
- 7–12 months: 220 micrograms
- 1–3 years: 340 micrograms

Good food sources include: beans, cocoa, kale, nutritional yeast, nuts, oysters, potatoes, prunes, spinach, whole grains.

Fluoride

When bonded chemically with calcium, fluoride helps strengthen teeth and maintain bone structure. It occurs, when bonded with sodium, in ocean water and most seafood. It doesn't arise in breast milk, so infants receive fluoride only through formula. Too much fluoride from birth through age 8 can lead to dental fluorosis, a mild condition that appears as faint white streaks on the teeth, often visible only to dentists or hygienists. The American Academy of Pediatric Dentistry and the CDC recommend no fluoride supplementation for infants younger than 6 months. The Food and Nutrition Board at the National Academy of Sciences established AIs, or Adequate Intakes for fluoride, which is used when evidence is insufficient to provide an RDA.

Recommended Daily Intake of Fluoride
- Pregnant and lactating mothers: 3,000 micrograms
- 0–6 months: 10 micrograms
- 7–12 months: 500 micrograms
- 1–3 years: 700 micrograms

Good food sources include: apples, bananas, cucumbers, potatoes, raisins, shellfish, spinach.

Iodine

This trace mineral produces thyroid hormones and plays a key role in fetal and skeletal development. Deficiency, even in the first trimester, can lead to hypothyroidism in mother and baby and result in cognitive impairment in the child.

Recommended Daily Intake of Iodine
- Pregnant mothers: 220 micrograms
- Lactating mothers: 290 micrograms

- 0–6 months: 110 micrograms
- 7–12 months: 130 micrograms
- 1–3 years: 90 micrograms

Good food sources include: chicken, dairy, eggs, fish, seaweed, shellfish.

Iron

This element, which comes in heme and non-heme dietary forms, helps produce red blood cells and energy. Plants contain non-heme iron, while poultry, meat, and seafood contain both kinds. As we've mentioned before, the WHO considers low iron the top nutritional deficiency and it's even common in developed countries like the United States. Up to 80 percent of the world's population may be iron deficient, and about 40 percent of children under age 5 suffer from anemia. Preterm or low-weight infants have a greater risk, and supplementation recommendations vary.[22] By age 6 months, babies have depleted all the iron they had at birth and received from their mothers. Deficiency can have significant effects on brain development and lead to future lower IQs, social withdrawal, delayed attention, and an increased risk of neurotoxicity.

Recommended Daily Intake of Iron
- Pregnant mothers: 27 milligrams
- Lactating mothers: 9 milligrams
- 0–6 months: 0.27 milligram
- 7–12 months: 11 milligrams
- 1–3 years: 7 milligrams

Good food sources include: asparagus, broccoli, Brussels sprouts, chickpeas, legumes, nuts, prunes, pumpkin seeds, raisins, spinach.

Magnesium

This mineral ensures normal nerve and muscle function. It also helps manage blood glucose levels and aids in energy production. Most people don't meet ideal levels, but true deficiency is rare.

Recommended Daily Intake of Magnesium
- Pregnant mothers: 350–360 milligrams
- Lactating mothers: 310–320 milligrams
- 0–6 months: 30 milligrams
- 7–12 months: 75 milligrams
- 1–3 years: 80 milligrams

Good food sources include: almonds, cashews, dairy, kale, legumes, pumpkin seeds, spinach, whole grains.

Manganese

This trace element helps form collagen, cartilage, and bones. Deficiency can lead to skeletal abnormalities, postural defects, and impaired growth. Too much, however, can cause a permanent neurological disorder. Children are more susceptible to manganese overdose because of the immaturity of their bile-elimination system. Dietary intake, including supplements, should never exceed 10 milligrams.

Recommended Daily Intake of Manganese

- Pregnant mothers: 2.0 milligrams
- Lactating mothers: 2.6 milligrams
- 0–6 months: 0.003 milligram
- 7–12 months: 0.6 milligram
- 1–3 years: 1.2 milligrams

Good food sources include: legumes, nuts, pineapple, shellfish, spinach, whole grains.

Molybdenum

This mineral processes proteins and genetic material. It also helps break down toxic substances that enter the body. Deficiency is exceptionally rare. Symptoms in infants include difficulty feeding, seizures, and atrophy of brain tissue.

Recommended Daily Intake of Molybdenum

- Pregnant and lactating mothers: 50 micrograms
- 0–6 months: 2 micrograms
- 7–12 months: 3 micrograms
- 1–3 years: 17 micrograms

Good food sources include: bananas, dairy, eggs, legumes, nuts, potatoes, poultry, whole grains.

Phosphorus

One of the most abundant minerals in the body, phosphorus occurs primarily in bones and teeth. It supports the growth, maintenance, and repair of all cells; is vital for the production of DNA and RNA; and filters kidney waste. Deficiency is rare, but excess levels can arise in people with severe kidney disease or calcium dysfunction.

Recommended Daily Intake of Phosphorus
- Pregnant and lactating mothers: 700 milligrams
- 0–6 months: 100 milligrams
- 7–12 months: 275 milligrams
- 1–3 years: 460 milligrams

Good food sources include: beans, dairy, eggs, fish, nuts, poultry, seeds, wheat germ.

Potassium

One of the most vital minerals in the body, potassium ensures the efficient functioning of cells, organs, muscles, and the digestive system. An electrolyte, it helps conduct electricity in the body. Deficiency, called hypokalemia, can cause weakness, cramps, constipation, and an abnormal heart rhythm.

Recommended Daily Intake of Potassium
- Pregnant mothers: 2,900 milligrams
- Lactating mothers: 2,800 milligrams
- 0–6 months: 400 milligrams
- 7–12 months: 860 milligrams
- 1–2 years: 2,000 milligrams

Good food sources include: apricots, bananas, broccoli, citrus, cucumbers, dairy, fish, legumes, melons, mushrooms, nuts, peas, potatoes, pumpkins, spinach, sweet potatoes, zucchini.

Selenium

This element helps regulate cell growth, keeps the thyroid healthy, and produces antioxidant enzymes. Selenium can be found in breast milk and in certain produce that draws it from the soil, so deficiency is rare, but large parts of the world have suboptimal levels. Signs of deficiency in infants include alopecia and delayed growth. However, while supplementation can help thyroid conditions, long-term, high-dose supplementation can lead to hair loss, fatigue, and gastrointestinal upset.

Recommended Daily Intake of Selenium
- Pregnant mothers: 60 micrograms
- Lactating mothers: 70 micrograms
- 0–6 months: 15 micrograms
- 7–12 months: 20 micrograms
- 1–3 years: 20 micrograms

Good food sources include: Brazil nuts, dairy, eggs, fish, poultry, shellfish, sunflower seeds, wheat germ, whole grains.

Sodium

This mineral—vital for cardiac, nerve, and muscle function—regulates blood pressure and blood volume. The most common form of intake occurs through sodium chloride, or table salt. Sodium occurs naturally in a wide variety of foods, including breast milk. Deficiency is rare, but according to the CDC, nearly all Americans consume too much. Given sodium's natural abundance, don't add table salt to foods for baby.

Recommended Daily Intake of Sodium
- Pregnant and lactating mothers: 1.5 grams
- 0–6 months: 120 milligrams
- 7–12 months: 370 milligrams
- 1–3 years: 1 gram

Good food sources include: dairy, nuts, olives, seafood, seeds.

Sulfur

The third most abundant mineral in the body, sulfur makes protein; builds and repairs DNA; aids the formation of connective tissues, such as ligaments, tendons, and cartilage; and helps bodies metabolize food. Intake occurs almost entirely through diet, with protein considered a wholly sufficient source.

Recommended Daily Intake of Sulfur
- Pregnant and lactating mothers: no adequate evaluation for RDI
- Don't give sulfur to an infant or child.

Good food sources include: arugula, broccoli, cauliflower, eggs, fish, garlic, kale, leeks, legumes, nuts, onions, poultry, radishes, seeds.

Zinc

This micronutrient plays a key role in cellular division, protein creation, immune function, and DNA production. Estimates suggest that 17 percent of the world's population may face a risk of zinc deficiency.[13] Inadequate levels can lead to anemia, impaired healing of wounds, poor motor function, diarrhea, and pneumonia.

Recommended Daily Intake of Zinc
- Pregnant mothers: 11 milligrams
- Lactating mothers: 12 milligrams
- 0–6 months: 2 milligrams

- 7–12 months: 3 milligrams
- 1–3 years: 3 milligrams

Good food sources include: apricots, asparagus, avocados, blackberries, blueberries, broccoli, cantaloupe, guava, hemp seeds, kiwifruit, legumes, mushrooms, peaches, peas, raspberries, shellfish, spinach, sweet potatoes.

Vitamins

The body doesn't synthesize most vitamins, or it does but in trace amounts.

Choline

During fetal development, choline impacts stem cell growth, promoting brain and spinal cord development. Many baby food products tout their choline content that helps the nervous system and brain function. Research suggests a direct link between folate and choline intakes.[14] Deficiencies can lead to neural tube defects.[15]

Recommended Daily Intake of Choline
- Pregnant mothers: 450 milligrams
- Lactating mothers: 550 milligrams
- 0–6 months: 125 milligrams
- 7–12 months: 150 milligrams
- 1–3 years: 200 milligrams

Good food sources include: almonds, broccoli, cauliflower, eggs, mushrooms, soybeans, wheat germ.

Folate

Called folic acid when synthetic and folate in food, this vital brain-growth vitamin aids in forming DNA, RNA, proteins, and blood cells. As with choline, deficiency can lead to neural defects. Risk factors include celiac disease, inflammatory bowel disease, and alcoholism.

Recommended Daily Intake of Folate
- Pregnant mothers: 600 micrograms
- Lactating mothers: 500 micrograms
- 0–6 months: 65 micrograms
- 7–12 months: 80 micrograms
- 1–3 years: 150 micrograms

Good food sources include: asparagus, broccoli, Brussels sprouts, spinach.

Biotin

Also called vitamin H after the German words *haar* and *haut*, meaning "hair" and "skin," it helps strengthen those body parts. The body doesn't store it, so you must consume it daily. Excess exits the body through urine. Biotin deficiency is rare because the body normally produces more than needed, but tube feeding or prolonged consumption of raw egg whites can cause deficiency. Symptoms include skin rash, dermatitis, and hair loss. Reports have suggested that a third of pregnant women develop a biotin deficiency, but the relationship between the deficiency and chances of congenital abnormalities remains unclear.[16]

Recommended Daily Intake of Biotin
- Pregnant mothers: 30 micrograms
- Lactating mothers: 35 micrograms
- 0–6 months: 5 micrograms
- 7–12 months: 6 micrograms
- 1–3 years: 8 micrograms

Good food sources include: bananas, spinach, sweet potatoes, cauliflower, eggs, legumes, nuts, whole grains.

Vitamin A

In food, we get our vitamin A via a red-pigment beta-carotene, which converts to vitamin A in the body. This chemical compound is essential for eye, skin, and bone health. Evidence shows that consuming beta-carotene from fruits and vegetables can lower the risk of cardiovascular disease, stroke, and some cancers. In one meta-analysis, vitamin A supplementation for 6 months decreased child mortality by 25 percent, and diarrhea mortality decreased by 30 percent.[17] Deficiency causes respiratory complications, vision issues, immunodeficiency, diarrhea, and a higher mortality risk from measles. High doses of vitamin A can prove toxic, but beta-carotene is safe. When the body's vitamin A stores are high, it doesn't convert beta-carotene, naturally avoiding a vitamin A overload.

Recommended Daily Intake of Vitamin A
- Pregnant mothers: 770 micrograms
- Lactating mothers: 1,300 micrograms
- 0–6 months: 400 micrograms
- 6–12 months: 500 micrograms
- 1–3 years: 300 micrograms

Good food sources include: apricots, broccoli, butternut squash, carrots, mangoes, peas, plums, red bell peppers.

Vitamin B$_1$

Also called thiamin, this vitamin helps convert food (including carbs) into energy; supports healthy muscles, skin, and hair; and maintains the nervous, muscular, and digestive systems. People who suffer from alcoholism, anorexia, or Crohn's disease have an increased risk for a B$_1$ deficiency, which can cause problems with the heart, circulatory system, and nerves.[18]

Recommended Daily Intake of Vitamin B$_1$

- Pregnant and lactating mothers: 1.4 milligrams
- 0–6 months: 0.2 milligram
- 7-12 months: 0.3 milligram
- 1–3 years: 0.5 milligram

Good food sources include: fish, legumes, peas, black beans, seeds, yogurt.

Vitamin B$_2$

This vitamin, known as riboflavin, helps convert food into energy. Deficiency commonly results from a lack of green vegetables.[19] When a lactating mother has a riboflavin deficiency, the breast milk also lacks the nutrient, making supplementation necessary for the infant.

Daily Recommended Intake of Vitamin B$_2$

- Pregnant mothers: 1.4 milligrams
- Lactating mothers: 1.6 milligrams
- 0–6 months: 0.3 milligram
- 7–12 months: 0.4 milligram
- 1–3 years: 0.5 milligram

Good food sources include: avocados, almonds, dairy, eggs, mushrooms, spinach.

Vitamin B$_3$

Also called niacin, this compound increases good cholesterol (HDL) and decreases triglycerides more effectively than prescription drugs. As a result, it reduces the risk of cardiovascular disease. Alcoholism is the most common cause of niacin deficiency, which causes problems with the nervous system, digestive system, and skin.

Recommended Daily Intake of Vitamin B$_3$
- Pregnant mothers: 18 milligrams
- Lactating mothers: 17 milligrams
- 0–6 months: 2 milligrams
- 7–12 months: 4 milligrams
- 1–3 years: 6 milligrams

Good food sources include: avocados, eggs, fish, mushrooms, peas, potatoes, poultry.

Vitamin B$_5$

This chemical compound, also known as pantothenic acid, helps manufacture energy, red blood cells, and hormones. It also helps the body absorb and use other vitamins, particularly B$_2$.[20] It supports a healthy digestive tract and synthesizes cholesterol. It occurs in a wide variety of food, making deficiency rare.

Recommended Daily Intake of Vitamin B$_5$
- Pregnant mothers: 6 milligrams
- Lactating mothers: 7 milligrams
- 0–6 months: 1.7 milligrams
- 7–12 months: 1.8 milligrams
- 1–3 years: 2 milligrams

Good food sources include: avocado, broccoli, dairy, eggs, mushrooms, nuts, oats, potatoes, seeds.

Vitamin B$_6$

This vitamin helps produce neurotransmitters, such as dopamine, GABA, norepinephrine, and serotonin, and it converts carbohydrates into energy. Deficiency, while rare, can cause seizures, abnormal brain waves, and other neurologic disorders.[21]

Recommended Daily Intake of Vitamin B$_6$
- Pregnant mothers: 1.9 milligrams
- Lactating mothers: 2 milligrams
- 0–6 months: 0.1–0.3 milligram
- 7–12 months: 0.3 milligram
- 1–3 years: 0.5 milligram

Good food sources include: bananas, beans, cantaloupe, chickpeas, fish, nuts, oranges, papayas, poultry.

Vitamin B$_{12}$

This compound supports the development and function of the brain, nervous system, and blood cells. The first 4 months of an infant's life represent the biggest risk for B$_{12}$ deficiency, which largely depends on how much the mother had during pregnancy.[22] B$_{12}$-deficient mothers (often vegetarians) who breastfeed may cause infant deficiencies as well.[23] Effects include stunted growth, muscular problems, and behavioral issues.[24]

Recommended Daily Intake of Vitamin B$_{12}$
- Pregnant mothers: 2.6 micrograms
- Lactating mothers: 2.8 micrograms
- 0–6 months: 0.4 microgram
- 7–12 months: 0.5 microgram
- 1–3 years: 0.9 microgram

Good food sources include: dairy, eggs, fish, fortified cereals, nutritional yeast, poultry, shellfish.

Vitamin C

The most famous antioxidant strengthens bones, teeth, and the nervous, circulatory, and immune systems. It assists in making collagen, which builds bone, blood vessels, tendons, cartilage, and skin. Deficiency, while rare, can cause scurvy, aaaarrrr matey.[25]

Recommended Daily Intake of Vitamin C
- Pregnant mothers: 85 milligrams
- Lactating mothers: 120 milligrams
- 0–6 months: 40 milligrams
- 7–12 months: 50 milligrams
- 1–3 years: 15 milligrams

Good food sources include: broccoli, Brussels sprouts, cauliflower, citrus, kiwifruit, mangoes, plums, potatoes, red bell peppers, strawberries, tomatoes.

Vitamin D

This compound acts as a hormone and maintains calcium levels, making it crucial for skeletal development. You also need it to absorb calcium from food.[26] Our bodies synthesize it from sunlight exposure, so winter months can give rise to deficiencies. Dietary sources are few. If breastfeeding mothers don't take vitamin D supplements during pregnancy, breastfed infants likely will require supplementation. Formula-fed infants don't need supplementation because producers fortify formula with it.

Recommended Daily Intake of Vitamin D
- Pregnant and lactating mothers: 15 micrograms
- 0–12 months: 10 micrograms
- 1–3 years: 15 micrograms

Good food sources include: eggs, fish, mushrooms, beef liver, cheese.

Vitamin E

Another antioxidant, vitamin E promotes immune, blood cell, and metabolic functions. Deficiency can occur when the body doesn't absorb fat properly. Crohn's disease, cystic fibrosis, and surgery are risk factors, as are infants who have low birth weights or drink unfortified formula.

Recommended Daily Intake of Vitamin E
- Pregnant mothers: 15 milligrams
- Lactating mothers: 19 milligrams
- 0–6 months: 4 milligrams
- 7–12 months: 5 milligrams
- 1–3 years: 6 milligrams

Good food sources include: almonds, legumes, pumpkin, red bell peppers, seeds, spinach, wheat germ.

Vitamin K

One of the most essential micronutrients, vitamin K is fat soluble and helps facilitate the clotting of blood. Deficiencies, a rarity, can cause bruising or bleeding. It doesn't pass adequately through breast milk. Formula contains high amounts of it, however, so deficiency in formula-fed babies is rare.

Recommended Daily Intake of Vitamin K
- Pregnant mothers: 75 micrograms
- Lactating mothers: 90 micrograms
- 0–6 months: 2 micrograms
- 7–12 months: 2.5 micrograms
- 1–3 years: 30 micrograms

Good food sources include: broccoli, Brussels sprouts, cauliflower, eggs, fish, kale, lettuce, spinach, blueberries, figs.

Fatty Acids

Omega-3s found in food play a huge role in neural and visual development and function, especially during pregnancy, lactation, and infancy. They also can resolve neurological and dermatological abnormalities.

Omega-6 fatty acids, which mostly come from vegetable oils and meats, fight inflammation, improve skin health, and promote immune function. Always try to maintain a healthy balance between omega-6 and omega-3 acids. The recommended ratio falls into a range between 2:1 and 4:1, omega-6 to omega-3. Western diets typically lack sufficient omega-3 and feature an excessive ratio of omega-6 to omega-3, which can lead to cancer, cardiovascular disease, and inflammatory disease.

Vitamins and Minerals Together

Some micronutrients can affect one another.

Calcium, Vitamin D, and Vitamin K_2

Vitamin D, an important nutrient for good health, can be synthesized from sun exposure. Some people take vitamin D supplements, however, which can affect calcium mobility. Taking vitamin D orally creates a higher demand for vitamin K_2, a partner in strengthening bone and promoting cardiovascular health. Calcium, recommended for brittle bones with the help of vitamin D, can make significant improvements.

Folic Acid, Thiamine, and Vitamin C

Thiamine has a major impact on the stability of folic acid. Vitamin C decreases folic acid levels, and in tests vitamin C cut the half-life of thiamine in half.

Iodine and Vitamin A

This mineral-vitamin combo helps with hypothyroidism. Children who took iodine-enriched salt along with vitamin A supplements showed a decrease in the concentration of their thyroid-stimulating hormone.[27]

Iron and Vitamin C

Vitamin C helps the body absorb iron. Broccoli, strawberries, red peppers, spinach, sweet potatoes, and tomatoes are rich in vitamin C. For maximum nutrition, pair them with iron-rich foods, such as legumes, potatoes, and dark leafy greens.

Kitchen Staples

No one is more strapped for time, energy, and sleep than a new parent. Once the casseroles and onesies stop showing up on your doorstep, you likely will have little motivation to explore grocery store shelves. That's why we assembled this list, to help you through those grueling first months. These ingredients are easy to handle, provide the energy required to get you and your little one through the day, and keep you both fuller longer. If you're breastfeeding, you need to ingest lots of vital nutrients. By eating the rainbow (page 44), you will familiarize your baby with diverse flavors, which can make it easier to introduce solids later. We recommend keeping the following ingredients on hand.

Almond Flour

When it comes to flour, almond takes the crown. Almond flour has lots of antioxidants as well as vitamin E. It tastes slightly sweet, which comes in handy for baking, especially for little ones, and it's gluten-free. Use it as a thickening agent for sauces, gravies, and soups or as a 1:1 substitute for all-purpose flour in pancakes, muffins, or cookies.

Bananas

These botanical berries (fleshy fruit, no pit, made by one flower containing one ovary) are easy on the stomach, naturally sweet, and packed with fiber and potassium. They're also convenient during early parenthood because you can eat them one-handed. Blend them into a smoothie, chop them onto some oatmeal, or slice them into a peanut butter sandwich. Yum!

Beans

While not a fruit, these members of the legume family are indeed magical. When little ones start solids, they often become constipated. Beans have loads of fiber, which makes them a great choice for blocked-up bébés. Beans increase feelings of fullness, lower cholesterol, and help maintain a healthy gut biome. Their protein content also makes them a terrific meat substitute. Add them to chilis, stews, and salads.

Beets

This protective and delicious root veggie has lots of antioxidants, which keep the body's free radicals in check. Beets also contain betaine that helps with cell reproduction, liver function, and removing toxins from the body.[28]

95

Bell Peppers

Also botanically berries, bell peppers have more vitamin C than oranges and provide an excellent source of vitamin A, potassium, folic acid, and fiber. Chop them into salads, slice them into burritos, or dip them in hummus.

Blueberries

Moms who recently have given birth should eat at least 2 servings of fruit per day. Blueberries contain lots of antioxidants and healthy low-glycemic carbs, keeping you fuller longer while keeping your energy levels high.

Broccoli

Prepping this green goodie is convenient and simple for new parents, requiring only steaming or chopping. Dip raw florets into hummus, yogurt ranch dressing, or tzatziki. You also can add broccoli to creamy soups, pasta, or homemade pizza.

Carrots

Carrots increase milk production and provide much-needed energy for sleep-deprived caregivers. Eat them steamed or raw as a handy snack.

Chia Seeds

Small and mighty, chia seeds offer a generous helping of fiber, protein, and omega-3s (healthy fats!). Mix them into dips, jam, oatmeal, or smoothies; bake them into bread or muffins; or sprinkle them on salads.

Flaxseed

With a mild flavor and crunchy texture, flaxseed is a nutritious, versatile ingredient. A great way to use it is as an egg substitute. Combine 1 tablespoon ground flaxseed and 3 tablespoons water, let the mixture sit for 5 minutes, and you have the equivalent of an egg substitute. For an easy nutrient boost, toss a tablespoon of ground flaxseed into a smoothie, pancake batter, or overnight oats.

Greens

Keep dark, leafy greens, such as collard greens, kale, spinach, or Swiss chard, on hand for salads, sandwiches, smoothies, or a cooked side dish.

Lentils

Like beans, lentils belong to the legume family. They have lots of protein, iron, and zinc, making them particularly helpful for vegans, vegetarians, or anyone looking to cut down on eating meat. Add these hearty little nuggets to dips, pasta, salads, soups, or stews.

Mushrooms

Incredible, edible mushrooms are one of the few plants that contain a good amount of vitamin D, which, like Sheryl Crow, they soak up from the sun. The level of vitamin D depends on the mushroom variety and how it was cultivated. Morels and chanterelles grow outside, so they pack a good dose. Good grocery-store selections include shiitake and button mushrooms.

Nutritional Yeast

Boasting an earthy, cheesy flavor, this versatile fungus is high in protein, low in fat, and nutrient dense. Add it to scrambled eggs, mix it into a vegan cheese sauce, sprinkle it on popcorn, or stir it into a soup (Angela affectionately refers to nutritional yeast flakes as fish food for her kids.) Not all manufacturers fortify nutritional yeast with B_{12}, so double-check the label.

Oats

This gluten-free whole grain is brimming with fiber, antioxidants, iron, potassium, and B vitamins. Use oats to make oatmeal (cooked or overnight), granola bars, muffins, or lactation cookies.

Quinoa

Rice often contains heavy metals, so quinoa is one of our favorite gluten-free substitutes. A complete protein, it contains all 20 amino acids that our bodies need. Add quinoa to cookies, pancakes, scrambles, and muffins, or just simmer it on the stovetop and enjoy it on its own.

Spirulina

This dark green dust packs a mighty punch. A little of this edible blue-green algae goes a long way in smoothies and other dishes. It has great antioxidant and anti-inflammatory properties, especially for the brain. It's also solid for vitamin B_{12} and protein.

Essential Tools

Babies need a lot of stuff—or so baby registries want you to believe. Sure, the first-time nesting vibe is real and some of the stuff is too cute to pass up, but most new parents quickly learn that you don't need 50+ onesies in much the same way that you don't need a million tools to make your own baby food. We recommend the following items for starting solids the simple way. Look for items that contain no BPA, lead, phthalates, or PVC.

Cup Cube Freezer Trays

Meal prep is part of the game. With strong-frame or spill-free freezer trays, you easily can transfer blends, soups, smoothies, and more to the freezer. Buy several and make sure that they come with snap-on lids, which make for easy stacking and protect against funky freezer odors or spillage. When you're ready to serve, just pop out the preportioned food cubes. Some trays even have measurements on the side so you know exactly how much you're serving. Most cubes come in 1 cup (8 ounce) portions and are dishwasher safe.

Food Processor

You don't need a fancy appliance to blend steamed vegetables. Some people like the all-in-one convenience of a combo steamer and processor, but for others it creates a big mess and can complicate the process. We like a basic, simple food processor to make hummus, other delicious dips, soups, and more. Just make sure the lid is secured tightly before you turn it on; otherwise, you'll be wearing dinner instead of eating it. Then just pop the top off, rinse, and clean. More advanced processors come with multiple blades, but almost all models can chop, mince, mash, and purée.

Glass Storage Containers with Lids

These are better than your parents' Tupperware because they come in all shapes and sizes, you can put hot food in them without fear of chemicals leeching into your little one's lunch, and you can see what's inside without having to open every single one to find what you want. Get lots of these in various sizes so you can nest them to save space in the cupboard. Also make sure the lids are dishwasher safe.

Ice Cream Scoop

This tool isn't 100 percent essential, but it makes portioning much easier. Once baby hits 11 months, your little one will be able to eat disk-shaped finger foods. Instead of getting your mitts all messy, use an ice cream scoop to dole out morsels. If you can, spring for one that comes with a trigger, which makes the process even easier.

Immersion Blender

Also called a stick blender, this handy tool makes quick work of small amounts of food. Plug it in, immerse the blades in the ingredients—particularly if they have a high water content—and watch solids transform before your very eyes.

Sieve

Depending on texture preferences and the age of your little one, you may want to de-chunk your sauces, soups, smoothies, and purées. The holes in a regular strainer are too large to filter seeds and small pieces of rind, so you'll need something with a finer mesh. A sieve is also great for rinsing quinoa, dried peas, lentils, beans, and pasta.

Steamer Basket

You don't need anything fancy, just a simple metal basket that goes over a pot of boiling water and has a lid. The rising steam cooks your veggies or other goodies. You can cook just about anything in a steamer basket, and the benefits are multifold. Steaming preserves nutrients, such as vitamin C and B vitamins, which regular cooking can damage. For example, boiling broccoli may cause it to lose 50 percent or more of its vitamin C.[29]

PART TWO

Recipes & Feeding Guides

Nutrient Highlights for the First 1,000 Days

Alpha-linolenic acid (fatty acids): an essential omega-3 fatty acid, plays a critical role in cell membrane formation and brain health.

Calcium: is a key mineral for the formation of strong bones and teeth. In infants, calcium is especially vital for building bone density.

Folate: helps support infants' rapidly growing cells and tissues as well as overall blood health and brain health.

Iron: is an essential mineral that is found in every red blood cell. It helps carry oxygen to the brain, making it vital for the brain.

Protein: is converted to amino acids, and then becomes all kinds of tissue, such as bones and muscles.

Vitamin A: Supports vision. helps break down free radicals, promotes cell production, and helps keep skin cells firm and healthy.

Vitamin D: is best known for building strong, healthy bones, and promoting good sleep.

Zinc: This mineral is relied upon by many processes in the body, including ones that impact growth, metabolism, and immunity.

In the first half of this book, we did some myth-busting, notably that food before 1 is *not* just for fun. As adults, we tend to believe that kids have their whole lives to worry about what they eat, but it turns out the opposite holds true, particularly during the first 1,000 days, the most critical window for nutrition and development.

Nutrition fuels growth. You or your partner choked down those giant horse pills during pregnancy because your baby needs extra nutrition during this key window. But a child's key nutritional needs don't end at birth. They continue through age 2. Certain nutrients play an outsized role during this window, and some are more important based on your child's stage of development, including folate and iron. Thousands of scientific papers focus on this essential time frame, and we even pivoted our careers to found Yumi to help people with it.

The science behind the first 1,000 days underscores Yumi's Milestone Plan, a best-selling program designed by nutritionists and approved by pediatricians. Following those milestones, the dishes that follow appear in order of baby's age—starting with pregnancy meals and ending with toddler fare—then by meal order, then total time. To help you focus on the right nutrients at the right time, we've labeled the recipes with 10 badges: Mama, Brain, Heart, Bones, Muscles, Eyes, Skin, Tummy, Immunity, and Sleep. Each dish contains vital amounts of certain nutrients essential for the various badge functions.

Now let's get cooking!

Pregnancy Dishes

MAMA FOOD

Just as plants need nutrient-rich soil to grow and multiply, our bodies need nourishment for themselves and to create new bodies. In the beginning, we pay so much attention to planning and preparing for babies that we often forget to feed ourselves. It happens to every new parent, but you can't ignore that your body needs fuel. The recipes in this section will help you get the nutrition that both of you need.

Mama Dragon Fruit Smoothie  0+

YIELD: 5 cups   PREP: 4 minutes
BLEND: 2 minutes   TOTAL: 6 minutes

Dragon fruit provides a healthy dose of nutrients for a pregnant woman and gives necessary nutritive elements for the child's growth. Taste training starts in utero. Dragon fruit is an amazing first single-ingredient food for babies 6+ months, so why not expose them early? Dragon fruit, a great source of healthy monounsaturated fat, provides fiber for constipation relief and is rich in B vitamins for healthy neural-tube development.

1 frozen banana (140 grams)

1½ cups (340 grams) dragon fruit, cubed (can be frozen)

1 tablespoon (10 grams) chia seed or flaxseed

½ cup (95 grams) blueberries (can be frozen)

½ cup (118 milliliters) almond milk or plant milk of choice

1. Combine all ingredients in a blender.

2. Pulse on high for 2 minutes.

3. Drink immediately.

NOTE: For a thinner smoothie, add an extra ½ cup of your plant milk of choice.

106

Broccoli Soup

YIELD: 4 cups (945 milliliters)   **PREP: 15 minutes**
COOK: 5 minutes   **TOTAL: 20 minutes**

New moms deserve a crown, so why not a broccoli crown? Some breastfeeding mamas worry that broccoli will make baby gassy. But the carbs in broccoli that cause gas can't transfer to the milk supply. We love a three-ingredient meal, but we *really* love anything that you can throw in a pot and make this fast. We also love meals that freeze well and that friends can make in bulk. This recipe is foolproof, even for people who burn toast. This soup contains a ton of vitamin A, vitamin C, calcium, fiber, potassium, and protein.

1 tablespoon sea salt

4 cups (340 grams) broccoli florets (2 broccoli crowns)

1½ cups (355 milliliters) vegetable (or chicken) stock

1   Bring a large pot of water to a boil. Add the sea salt.

2   Add the broccoli to the water, letting it boil for about 3 minutes, or until soft.

3   Add the broccoli and stock to a blender and blend until smooth.

4   Add any desired garnishes. We suggest goat cheese, walnuts, olive oil, or black pepper.

Mushroom Soup

YIELD: 3½ cups (828 milliliters) **PREP: 20 minutes**
COOK: 40 minutes **TOTAL: 1 hour**

Some specialists have found that breastfeeding mothers who increase their intake of beta-glucan–rich foods can increase their milk supply. Reishi, shiitake, maitake, shimeji, and oyster mushrooms have the highest beta-glucan content in the mushroom family.

1 tablespoon olive oil

1 small onion, diced

1 pound (453 grams) reishi, shiitake, maitake, shimeji, or oyster mushrooms (or a combination)

½ teaspoon garlic powder

½ tablespoon fresh thyme or 1 teaspoon dried

½ teaspoon oregano

½ teaspoon basil

2 cups (472 milliliters) vegetable broth

1 cup (236 milliliters) coconut milk, plus extra for drizzling

1½ tablespoons arrowroot powder

Parsley for garnish

Salt and pepper to taste

1. To a large pot over medium-high heat, add the olive oil and diced onion. Sauté the onion pieces until they become translucent, 5 to 7 minutes.

2. Add the mushrooms, garlic powder, thyme, oregano, and basil. Cook for 10 minutes, stirring occasionally.

3. Add the broth and bring to a boil. Cover, reduce heat, and simmer for 10 minutes.

4. Add the coconut milk and simmer for 5 minutes.

5. Mix the arrowroot powder with 1 tablespoon water. Add it to the soup and simmer for 5 more minutes, until the soup thickens.

6. Drizzle with extra coconut milk, garnish with parsley, and season with salt and pepper.

Greens & Grains Lactation Salad

YIELD: 5½ cups (1.28 kilograms)   PREP: 45 minutes
COOK: 20 minutes   TOTAL: 1 hour 5 minutes

New mommas need a lot of extra nutrients. As parents, we provide our babies with all the nutrients they need. In the first few months of life, we are their only source of nutrition, so to provide them with the best, we need to give ourselves the best, including this amazing salad.

Spinach provides fiber and iron, quinoa provides protein, and red rice adds antioxidants and phytochemicals. The oranges, apricots, and pistachios give it a richer profile and brighter flavor. You're going to love this salad as much as we do!

GRAINS

1 cup (150 grams) quinoa

1 cup (160 grams) Camargue red rice

1 tablespoon extra virgin olive oil

1 small onion (130 grams), thinly sliced

Pink Himalayan salt and freshly ground black pepper to taste

1   Preheat the oven to 375°F.

2   Bring 2 medium saucepans of salted water to a boil.

3   Cook the quinoa and rice in separate pots, according to package directions.

4   Once the grains have cooked, drain them and spread them on baking sheets to cool.

5   On another baking sheet, roast the pistachios in the oven for 5 minutes, then let cool.

6   In a medium skillet over medium heat, add 1 tablespoon olive oil and the onion and season with salt and pepper. Cover and cook, stirring occasionally, until golden brown, about 10 minutes. Let cool.

continues

DRESSING

1½ teaspoons finely grated orange zest (from 1 orange)

⅓ cup (80 milliliters) fresh orange juice (from 1 orange)

1 tablespoon fresh lemon juice

1 garlic clove, minced

3 tablespoons extra virgin olive oil

OTHER COMPONENTS

1 cup (130 grams) pistachios, chopped

½ cup (100 grams) dried apricots, quartered

1 orange, supreme (70 grams)

4 green onions, greens only, finely chopped

2 cups (50 grams) spinach

7 For the dressing, combine the orange zest, orange juice, lemon juice, garlic, and 3 tablespoons olive oil. Season with salt and pepper to taste.

8 In a large bowl, combine the quinoa, rice, onion, apricots, orange segments, pistachios, green onions, and spinach. Toss well.

NOTE: If you can't find red rice, use brown rice instead.

Veggie Lentil Coconut Curry

YIELD: 5½ cups PREP: 15 minutes
COOK: 40 minutes TOTAL: 55 minutes

Curry, one of the world's most comforting flavors, immediately conjures up favorite dishes from Thailand or India. Typically it consists of turmeric, coriander, cardamom, cumin, sweet basil, and red pepper and offers a healthy way to bring dynamic flavor to vegetarian and vegan dishes. Turmeric has become increasingly popular as an anti-inflammatory, while cumin aids in digestion and also provides a bit of iron.

Carrots are rich in fiber, beta-carotene, vitamin K, and manganese. These minerals contribute to healthy bone structure and vision. Celery adds an extra dose of vitamin K and folate. Warm and soothing vegetable broth also has lots of vitamins and minerals. The coconut milk adds a creamy texture and healthy fats to help you feel satiated. Lentils and brown rice add additional fiber and nutrients to an incredibly nourishing meal.

continues

1 small onion, diced

**1 tablespoon olive
or coconut oil**

**4 carrots (290 grams),
peeled and diced**

**3 celery stalks (100
grams), diced**

**4 cups (950 millili-
ters) sodium-free
vegetable broth**

**1 cup (237 milliliters)
coconut milk**

**½ cup (75 grams)
green lentils**

**½ cup (75 grams) long-
grain brown rice**

2 teaspoons curry powder

¼ teaspoon salt

¼ teaspoon pepper

1. In a large saucepan over medium-high heat, combine the diced onion and olive or coconut oil. Sauté for 2 minutes, until the onions begin to soften.

2. Add in the diced carrots and celery and sauté for 3 to 4 more minutes, until all the vegetables have begun to soften.

3. Pour in the vegetable broth and coconut milk and cook for 2 to 3 minutes.

4. Add the green lentils, long-grain brown rice, curry powder, salt, and pepper. Stir well.

5. Over low-medium heat with a lid on the pot, simmer the mixture for 25 to 30 minutes, stirring occasionally, until the veggies, lentils, and rice become soft and tender.

6. Allow to cool.

NOTES: Spice up this dish, if you like heat, with red chili flakes or cayenne pepper. We encourage you to double this recipe so that you have time-saving leftovers for the whole week.

Mother Borscht

YIELD: 1 cup (250g)   PREP: 10 minutes
COOK: 20 minutes 30 seconds   TOTAL: 30 minutes 30 seconds

Breastfeeding women have higher needs for many nutrients, including iron. Spinach contains lots of key vitamins and minerals, including iron, potassium, beta-carotene, and vitamins C, E, and K. Beets provide fiber, vitamin C, magnesium, and potassium. Coconut milk adds a sweet note to this blend and adds healthy fats. Ground flaxseed meal adds omega-3s and more good fiber.

1½ cup beets, peeled and diced (4 large beets)

1½ cups (50 grams) spinach, packed

2 tablespoons coconut milk

1 tablespoon ground flaxseed meal

Sour cream and herbs or spices of choice for garnish (optional)

1   Add the beets to a steamer basket and steam them for 15 minutes.

2   Add the spinach to the steamer and steam for 5 more minutes.

3   Add the steamed beets, spinach, coconut milk, and ground flaxseed meal to a food processor.

4   Blend until the mixture is smooth, adding more coconut milk if necessary.

5   Garnish with sour cream and herbs or spices of choice.

6   Serve immediately.

NOTES: You can freeze this borscht in freezer-safe glass containers for up to 2 months. When reheating, place it in a microwave-safe glass dish and microwave in increments of 30 seconds to 1 minute until it heats all the way through.

Veggie Quinoa Chili

**YIELD: 8½ cups   PREP: 15 minutes
COOK: 45 minutes   TOTAL: 1 hour**

We love one-pot meals for new parents. Inspired by Yumi's chili purée, this dish is packed with nutrients, so you can feel good about your whole family eating it and feel revived when you eat it yourself. You can dress up this dish in plenty of ways. Consider avocado, sour cream, shredded cheese, ground turkey, ground beef, or other favorite toppings. Double the recipe for grab-and-go lunches all week long.

CHILI

1 onion, diced

4 cloves garlic, minced

1 tablespoon olive oil

1 cup (170 grams) cooked quinoa

One 28-ounce (794-gram) can diced tomatoes

One 15-ounce (425-gram) can tomato sauce

One 4.5-ounce (127-gram) can green chiles

One 15-ounce (425-gram) can kidney beans

One 15-ounce (425-gram) can white beans

1 cup (130 grams) frozen corn

2½ teaspoons smoked paprika

2 teaspoons cumin

2 teaspoons dried parsley

1 teaspoon chili powder

½ teaspoon turmeric

½ teaspoon salt

½ teaspoon black pepper

TOPPINGS

Sour cream

Shredded Cheddar cheese

Fresh cilantro

Diced avocado

Black pepper

1   In a large stockpot over medium-high heat, combine the diced onion, minced garlic, and olive oil. Sauté the onion and garlic for 5 to 8 minutes, until the onions become soft and translucent.

2   Add the quinoa, diced tomatoes, tomato sauce, green chiles, kidney beans, and white beans. Mix until well combined and simmer for 5 minutes.

3   Add the frozen corn, smoked paprika, cumin, dried parsley, chili powder, turmeric, salt, and black pepper. Mix until well combined.

4   Allow the mixture to simmer for 20 to 30 minutes, until the flavors combine well.

5   Scoop the chili into bowls, add the toppings of your choice, and serve immediately.

Sleepy Tea 0+

YIELD: 6 cups PREP: 5 minutes
STEEP: 15 to 20 minutes TOTAL: 20 to 25 minutes

If the idea of deep sleep sounds like a fantasy, you need our doula-recommended Sleepy Tea. A cup of this is great not only for bedtime, but it also helps relax and restore a "fried" nervous system—which often results from raising a tiny person—healing the body on a cellular level from deep stress. In other words, it will help you chill out.

The beauty of this tea is that the ingredients are effective enough for an adult yet gentle enough for a child. Taken around bedtime, it won't make you drowsy but rather will help relax you enough to allow for restorative sleep. If you're breastfeeding, this tea will provide safe levels of relaxation through your milk to your little one.

1 tablespoon linden
1 tablespoon passionflower
1 tablespoon skullcap
1 teaspoon holy basil or tulsi
1 teaspoon lemon balm
1 teaspoon lavender

1 Combine the herbs into a bowl and store in an airtight jar.

2 To serve, add 2 teaspoons of herbs to a tea ball or reusable muslin tea bag.

3 Pour 2 cups of boiling water on top and steep for 15 to 20 minutes.

Lactation Cookies 0+

YIELD: 20 cookies   PREP: 10 minutes
COOK: 15 minutes   TOTAL: 25 minutes

Cookies to increase breast milk? It sounds too good to be true, and often it is. Several shelf-stable brands on the market teem with refined sugars. But with a little creativity in the kitchen, you can make a healthy and effective version. The magic in these cookies comes down to two ingredients: oats and brewer's yeast. They both are galactagogues, a fancy word for foods that increase the flow of mother's milk. Grass-fed butter increases the fat content of breast milk, providing your baby with vital brain nutrients, such as DHA. These hearty cookies contain B vitamins, minerals, protein, and healthy fats, making them an excellent snack for nursing mothers.

Bake them when you get a craving or freeze the dough for up to 3 months. Just make sure to bake extra because the whole family is going to love these. (They won't make men lactate, but you don't need to say that if you don't want to share.)

continues

2 cups (180 grams) organic rolled oats

¼ cup (32 grams) tapioca or arrowroot flour

¼ cup (30 grams) brewer's yeast

1 teaspoon baking powder

½ teaspoon baking soda

½ teaspoon sea salt

½ cup (113 grams) grass-fed butter, room temperature

½ cup (40 grams) organic coconut sugar

2 eggs, room temperature

½ teaspoon vanilla extract

½ cup (120 grams) almond butter

3 tablespoons raw honey

1. Preheat the oven to 350°F.

2. Add the rolled oats to a high-speed blender or food processor and blend or process until the oats become oat flour.

3. Mix all the dry ingredients together in a large bowl. Set aside.

4. In a kitchen mixer with a paddle attachment or with a hand mixer, cream the grass-fed butter and sugar together at high speed for 2 to 3 minutes.

5. Beat the eggs and vanilla into the mixture at medium speed until just combined. Scrape down the sides of the bowl.

6. Add 1 cup of the dry ingredients into the mixer and mix until just combined.

7. Add the almond butter and raw honey and mix until incorporated. Scrape down the sides of the bowl.

8. Mix in the rest of the dry ingredients until fully incorporated. Gently add in mix-ins, if desired.

9. Grease a cookie sheet with coconut oil. Form small, flat balls of dough, about an inch wide, and distribute evenly on the cookie sheet.

10. Bake for 14 to 16 minutes. The cookies are done when they have browned slightly.

11. Remove from the oven and transfer cookies to a cooling rack.

12. Serve warm or let cookies cool to room temperature.

NOTES: You can add endless mix-ins to this recipe. We enjoy shredded coconut, chocolate chips, dried cranberries, raisins, and a dash of pumpkin spice.

Also consider the following substitutions. If you're allergic to tree nuts, replace the almond butter with peanut butter, sunflower butter, or even tahini. For a vegan version, replace the butter with coconut oil and the honey with maple syrup.

6

Starting Solids

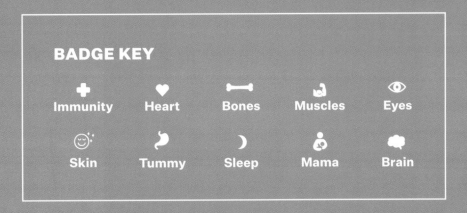

BADGE KEY

Immunity	Heart	Bones	Muscles	Eyes
Skin	Tummy	Sleep	Mama	Brain

Babies start solids with single-ingredient purées. Making them isn't rocket science, but it is important to understand how new foods influence developmental milestones. So much is happening that it can be hard to ensure your baby is getting essential nutrition. When in doubt, eat the rainbow! Once your baby has mastered eating single ingredients, move on to two-ingredient blends. These still have a thin texture but offer a great way to play with flavor and to make foods such as kale a bit more palatable.

Start solids with vegetable and fruit purées. Generally speaking, you want to steam and purée veggies. Some fruits are soft enough to mash without steaming or cooking, as indicated.

Raspberry Blend

YIELD: ½ cup (118 milliliters)   **PREP:** 1 minute
BLEND: 15 seconds   **TOTAL:** 1 minute 15 seconds

great for BREAKFAST

Sweet, bright raspberries are loaded with antioxidants and vitamin C, making them wonderful for strengthening your little one's immune system. They also contain loads of other vitamins and minerals, including magnesium, calcium, iron, folate, and vitamin B_6, all of which contribute to brain health and a good night's sleep.

6 ounces (170 grams) raspberries

1   Sample 1 or 2 berries to confirm they don't taste too tart, then give them a good rinse.

2   Add the raspberries and 1 tablespoon water to a blender. Blend until smooth, about 15 seconds.

3   If you want to remove the seeds, strain the purée.

4   Serve or freeze.

TOP ROW, L–R: Raspberry Blend, Blackberry Blend, Beet Blend
MIDDLE ROW, L–R: Broccoli Blend, Black Bean Blend, Dragon Fruit Blend
BOTTOM ROW, L–R: Pear Blend, Kale and Apple Blend, Squash and Pear Blend

Blackberry Blend

MONTH 6+

YIELD: ½ cup (118 milliliters) **PREP: 1 minute**
BLEND: 15 seconds **TOTAL: 1 minute 15 seconds**

great for
BREAKFAST

Blackberries are rich in calcium, a mineral essential for forming new bone tissue. They also contain four other bone-building minerals: copper, magnesium, manganese, and potassium. Best of all, new eaters love them!

**6 ounces (170 grams)
    blackberries**

1   Sample 1 or 2 berries to confirm they don't taste too tart, then give them a good rinse.

2   Add the blackberries and 1 tablespoon water to a blender. Blend until smooth, about 15 seconds.

3   If you want to remove the seeds, strain the purée.

4   Serve or freeze.

MILESTONE

At birth a baby has 300 bones in its cute little body. (Adults have 206.) As babies grow, malleable bones fuse together in a process called ossification.

Beet Blend

YIELD: 1 cup (240 milliliters) PREP: 5 minutes
COOK: 35 minutes 20 seconds TOTAL: 40 minutes 20 seconds

Beets contain betaine and choline, which work to regulate inflammation, contributing to overall heart health. Beets are also high in folate, which helps maintain a healthy heart.

4 beets (250 grams)

1 Trim the beet root and quarter the beets.

2 In a medium saucepan, add the beets and about 1½ cups water, enough so the beets are submerged partially.

3 Bring the water to a boil, then reduce the heat to low. Simmer for approximately 35 minutes.

4 Add the beets to a blender or food processor. Add 1 or 2 tablespoons of water if necessary. Pulse or blend until smooth.

5 Serve or freeze.

MILESTONE

Pop quiz! What's the largest organ in the human body? It's not your lungs or liver. It's your skin. For babies, the protective layer of tissue that coats the entire body, continues developing after birth. In the first year of life, baby's skin is much more sensitive than an older child's. From 3 to 12 months, it's more prone to infections and more vulnerable to toxins, which is why you should scrutinize the chemicals in products that might come into contact with their sweet cheeks.

133

Broccoli Blend

YIELD: 5 ounces **PREP: 5 minutes**
COOK: 5 to 8 minutes **TOTAL: 10 to 13 minutes**

great for LUNCH OR DINNER

Every brain needs a crown of green. It's simple really. Broccoli teems with brain-healthy nutrients such as lutein, folate, and beta-carotene. It also contains sulforaphane, a compound with antioxidant and anti-inflammation properties, which can help rebuild your brain. Post-partum, you probably feel like yours needs rebuilding. If so, try this recipe when you feed it to your little one.

1 broccoli floret (approximately 150 grams)
Olive oil

1 Fill a saucepan with 2 inches of water and place it over high heat.

2 Roughly chop the broccoli.

3 Make sure the water is steaming hot before adding the broccoli to a steamer basket.

4 Steam the broccoli until tender. Smaller florets need to steam for about 5 minutes, while larger florets take 6 minutes or more.

5 Transfer the cooked broccoli pieces into a blender or food processor and add a drizzle of olive oil. Purée 15 seconds, until smooth.

6 Allow to cool and serve or freeze.

NOTE: If you have one, you can use a rice maker with a steamer basket to make this blend.

Black Bean Blend

YIELD: 1½ cups (355 milliliters) **PREP: 1 minute**
BLEND: 15 seconds **TOTAL: 1 minute 15 seconds**

great for DINNER

Around the 6-month mark, your baby's iron stores begin to run low. Iron helps carry oxygen to the brain, making it one of the most important minerals for growth and development.

Black beans are a great plant-based source of iron.

One 15-ounce can (425 grams) organic black beans

1 Place the black beans into a large strainer and rinse them under cold water until the water runs clear.

2 Add the black beans and 1 tablespoon water to a blender. Blend for 15 seconds until smooth.

Dragon Fruit Blend (6+)

YIELD: 14 ounces (414 milliliters) **PREP: 2 minutes**
BLEND: 15 seconds **TOTAL: 2 minutes 15 seconds**

 great for **SNACKS** or **DESSERT**

Dragon fruit works with vitamin A to support healthy vision. It also looks really cool. Also high in fiber, prebiotics, and riboflavin, it promotes a healthy gut.

1 dragon fruit (460 grams)

1 Cut the dragon fruit in half and scoop out the pulp.

2 Add the pulp to a blender or food processor and blend it into a smooth purée.

3 Serve or freeze.

MILESTONE

At birth, babies can see only in black and white. At the 5-month mark, the world starts coming into sharp focus. By the start of month 6, bébés have developed all their primarily visual capabilities, including depth perception, color vision, fine acuity, and controlled eye movements. At this point, they can distinguish pastel colors, but don't worry—they won't be popping their collars . . . yet. Continue exposing your baby to books and toys with a wide range of hues to expand their awareness of color.

136

Pear Blend

MONTH
6+

YIELD: 1 cup (237 milliliters) **PREP: 5 minutes**
COOK: 10 minutes 15 seconds **TOTAL: 15 minutes 15 seconds**

great for
SNACKS OR DESSERT

Fiber is the indigestible part of plant foods—sometimes called "roughage"—that pushes through the digestive system, absorbing water along the way and easing bowel movements. Incorporating natural, fibrous foods into your baby's diet will ensure more happy toots and fewer tears. Plums are great, and so are pears.

2 Bartlett pears

1 Leaving the skins on, dice the pears and discard the cores.

2 Fill a medium pot with 2 inches of water and bring water to a simmer.

3 Add the diced pears to a steamer basket, place it in the pot, and cover.

4 Steam until soft, about 10 minutes.

5 Blend until smooth, about 15 seconds. Add 1 tablespoon water if necessary.

6 Allow to cool and serve or freeze.

NOTE: Bartlett pears tend to have thinner skins that blend more easily.

137

Kale and Apple Blend (MONTH 7+)

YIELD: 1 cup (236 milliliters)   PREP: 5 minutes
COOK: 12 minutes 30 seconds   TOTAL: 17 minutes 30 seconds

The health benefits of kale, the ultimate superfood, are too numerous to list. So we'll drop a lesser-known fact here: kale is rich in calcium, which is important for bone health—especially during childhood, when baby bodies are creating bone mass.

2 Fuji apples (260 grams), peeled, cored, and diced
½ cup (12 grams) loose kale

1   In a steamer, bring 2 inches of water to a boil.

2   Cover and steam the apples for 10 minutes.

3   Add the kale and steam for 2 more minutes.

4   Add the kale, apples, and 1 tablespoon water to a blender. Blend for 30 seconds, until smooth.

MILESTONE

At around 6 months, babes attempt to sit up. They will try and fail many times before they succeed. Always keep a few extra pillows nearby for when they plop over. The act of sitting signifies that your child has more control over the body's core muscles.

Squash and Pear Blend

YIELD: 2 cups (473 milliliters) **PREP: 10 minutes**
COOK: 25 minutes 30 seconds **TOTAL: 35 minutes 30 seconds**

great for
LUNCH

Kabocha squash, also known as Japanese pumpkin, looks golden-yellow, tastes delicious, and contains healthy doses of potassium, vitamin A, and vitamin B_{12}, among other amazing vitamins and minerals. It also has high amounts of folate and vitamin B_6, which contribute to a happy, healthy brain.

**1 small kabocha squash
(360 grams)**

1 Anjou pear (165 grams)

1. Peel the kabocha squash and cut it in half. Deseed and roughly chop it.

2. Core and quarter the pear.

3. In a steamer, bring about 2 cups of water to a boil. Steam the squash for 15 minutes.

4. Add the pears and continue steaming for 10 more minutes.

5. Toss the pears, squash, and ¼ cup (60 milliliters) water into a blender. Blend for 30 seconds.

6. Allow to cool and serve or freeze.

NOTE: If you can't find kabocha, substitute butternut or acorn squash. For a smoother blend, peel the pear.

Purple Sweet Potato and Blueberry Blend

YIELD: 2½ cups (591 milliliters)   **PREP: 10 minutes**
COOK: 30 minutes 30 seconds   **TOTAL: 40 minutes 30 seconds**

Japanese purple sweet potatoes are rich in vitamins, minerals, and antioxidants that are great for the immune system, especially those of 7-month-olds on the precipice of mouthing *everything*. (Remember, that's one of the signs that they're ready for solids!) Purple sweet potatoes don't taste as sweet as their better-known orange counterparts, which makes this pairing with blueberries a perfect combo for your little one's growing palate.

1 small purple sweet potato, peeled and roughly diced

6 ounces (170 grams) blueberries

1   Bring a small saucepan of water to a boil. Add the sweet potatoes and boil them for 25 to 30 minutes.

2   Toss the sweet potatoes, blueberries, and ½ cup (120 milliliters) water into a food processor or blender. Blend until smooth, about 30 seconds.

Spice It Up!

Does the monotony of baby food make your eyelids heavy? As much as you need those z's, your baby's food doesn't need to be a snooze. Once your baby has started solids successfully, here are a few simple ways to spice up those single-ingredient blends.

Pear: Pears are tasty, so is Greek yogurt. Put 'em together, and you have breakfast. Try adding a dash of cinnamon to this tasty concoction.

Sweet potato: 'Tis the season for a dash of fresh nutmeg and a little bit of chopped parsley. Simple, easy, happiness.

Black beans: A smidge of garlic powder increases immunity and heart strength. Oregano provides some flair.

Ahh, carrots: good for the eyes, good for the soul. Make them even better by adding some mushy peas into the mix or add a dash of paprika and cinnamon and give it a stir so baby can see carrots in a whole new way.

Applesauce

MONTH 7+

**YIELD: 4 cups (980 grams)   PREP: 25 minutes
COOK: 50 minutes   TOTAL: 1 hour 15 minutes**

great for
SNACKS or **DESSERT**

Your baby is sweet enough, which is why we make our applesauce with no added sugar. Instead, we use lucuma, a dried powder made from a green Peruvian fruit. A low-glycemic sweetener, it has a subtle maple flavor. It offers an excellent source of fiber, minerals, and vitamins, especially B_3. The cinnamon and nutmeg in this recipe will smell and taste like fall, but you and your little one can enjoy it any day of the year.

8 to 10 small apples, peeled, cored, and quartered

1 teaspoon lucuma

½ teaspoon cinnamon

½ teaspoon nutmeg

1   In a large pot over medium heat, add the quartered apples and 1½ cups (350 milliliters) water. Cover the pot with a lid and simmer for 20 to 30 minutes, until the apples have become soft.

2   Strain the apples and let cool.

3   Toss the apples, lucuma, cinnamon, and nutmeg into the blender. Blend until smooth.

4   Serve immediately or keep in the fridge for up to 1 week.

MILESTONE

As little ones move into the second 6 months of life, they need fiber to keep everything running smoothly. Between 6 months and 1 year, about 5 grams of fiber per day is standard. When it comes to fiber-rich foods to prevent or relieve constipation, think straight from the earth, the less processed the better.

Wee Explorers

MONTHS 8 TO 11

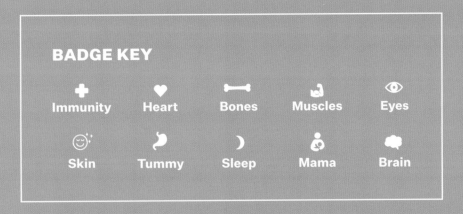

BADGE KEY

Immunity · Heart · Bones · Muscles · Eyes

Skin · Tummy · Sleep · Mama · Brain

Proper nutrition plays an essential role in the development of a child's muscular system. By now, your baby most likely is crawling all over the place. Some babies crawl as early as 7 months, while 9 months is the average, and some won't crawl until 11 months. Want to encourage your little one to crawl? Let your kiddo have lots of tummy time, which will help increase strength in those little arms and abdomen. You also can place a favorite toy or object slightly out of reach and encourage your little explorer to reach it.

On the move means in the mouth. At this age, everything your little one touches ends up in his or her mouth. That's how they learn about the world, and it's a good thing! Exposure to germs helps build a baby's immune system.

Apricot Turmeric Bowl

MONTH 8+

YIELD: 1 cup (237 milliliters)   PREP: 5 minutes
COOK: 30 minutes 30 seconds   TOTAL: 35 minutes 30 seconds

great for
BREAKFAST

Turmeric helps fight heavy metal toxicity because it contains curcumin, an important chemical that alleviates inflammation, acts as an antioxidant, regulates blood sugar, improves cell functionality, and supports digestive and brain health. Turmeric is safe for babies starting solids, and the body absorbs it best with other ingredients. That's why we've added it here, when your little one has graduated to single-ingredient blends.

2 apricots

½ banana

2 dates

½ teaspoon cinnamon

¼ teaspoon turmeric

¼ teaspoon freshly grated ginger

¼ teaspoon clove

1   Bring a small pot of water to a boil. Add the apricots whole and boil them for 30 minutes, until they start coming apart.

2   Rinse the apricots in cold water, then peel and de-stone them.

3   Add all the ingredients, plus 2 tablespoons water, to a food processor. Blend for 30 seconds, until smooth.

NOTES: For more advanced eaters, buckwheat makes a great hearty, healthy addition to this blend. This tasty, nutritious, fibrous whole grain keeps babies regular and packs more protein than quinoa and lots of magnesium.

TOP ROW, L–R: Apricot Turmeric Bowl, Cubano Blend
MIDDLE ROW, L–R: Veggie Soup, Squash and Greens Bowl
BOTTOM ROW, L–R: Ratatouille, Greens Smoothie

Cubano Blend

YIELD: 2 cups (480 grams)   **PASSIVE: 8 hours**
PREP: 2 hours   **PROCESSING: 5 minutes**
TOTAL: 10 hours 5 minutes

great for
LUNCH

Think it'll be hard to get your baby to eat beans and kale? Not with this recipe. The sweetness of the banana balances the bitterness of kale and beans, making it a great way to feed your baby plant-based protein along with all the superfood benefits of kale. See photo on page 146.

¼ **cup (40 grams) black beans, soaked overnight**

1 **banana (140 grams)**

2 **cups (164 grams) kale, stems removed and chopped**

¼ **cup (31 grams) quinoa**

1 **tablespoon flaxseed**

1   Bring 4 small pots of water to a boil. Add the black beans to one pot and reduce the heat to medium. Boil for 1 to 2 hours, until tender.

2   Add the quinoa to the second pot of boiling water and reduce the heat to a simmer. Cover and cook on low heat for 20 minutes.

3   In the third pot of boiling water, steam the kale for 15 minutes.

4   Cut off the ends of the banana and add it to the last pot of boiling water. Lower the temperature to medium and cook for 10 minutes.

5   Strain the black beans, banana, and kale, then add them to a food processor with the quinoa. Pulse everything together until smooth while gradually adding the flaxseed.

MILESTONE

As babies learn to crawl, they have a harder time sleeping during the night. That's because motor skills often develop during REM sleep. Seeing them crawl in their sleep? Cute! But it's less cute when it wakes them up. At this age, maintaining healthy magnesium levels can lead to deeper, sounder sleep. Magnesium supports restorative sleep by maintaining healthy levels of GABA, a neurotransmitter.

Raspberry Chia Jam

YIELD: 2½ cups   PREP: 5 minutes
COOK: 20 minutes   TOTAL: 25 minutes

great for
SNACKS or **DESSERT**

Chia seeds are small but mighty. One of the top plant-based sources of protein, they also contain calcium, phosphorus, magnesium, manganese, copper, iron, and zinc.

**1 pound (454 grams)
   frozen raspberries**

**3 tablespoons (125 grams)
   date paste**

1½ tablespoons maple syrup

½ tablespoon beet powder

1 teaspoon vanilla extract

⅛ to ¼ cup chia powder

1   In a saucepan over high heat, place all ingredients except chia powder and bring to a boil.

2   Let the fruit mixture boil for 15 minutes.

3   Take the jam off the heat. If you want to remove the raspberry seeds, run the warm mixture through a cheesecloth or sieve.

4   Mix in the chia powder and allow to cool.

NOTES: Chia powder thickens the jam to the perfect consistency, not too thick, not too runny. If you want something a little thinner, we suggest ⅛ cup of chia powder. If you have a food processor, you can grind chia seeds to a powder.

149

Veggie Soup

**YIELD: 4 cups   PREP: 15 minutes
COOK: 20 minutes   TOTAL: 35 minutes**

This dish features lots of all-star ingredients: broccoli, carrots, sweet potato, and acorn squash, all high in vitamin A, essential for your baby's immune system and cell growth. The shining stars of the group are the broccoli and carrots. Their magnesium content increases your bundle of joy's energy, digestion, and heart health. With nutritional yeast as a great source of B-complex vitamins, this meal will keep your baby sated until naptime. See photo on page 146.

2 carrots (approximately 185 grams)

½ broccoli crown (approximately 155 grams)

1 small sweet potato (approximately 185 grams)

½ acorn squash (approximately 142 grams)

2 tablespoons nutritional yeast

1   Wash and dry the fresh produce.

2   Over high heat, bring a large pot of water to a boil.

3   Peel the carrots and chop them into 1-inch cubes.

4   Remove and discard the broccoli leaves. Cut the bottom off the stem and shave the stem. Then cut the stem free from the head. Cut the stem into rounds and cut the head into individual florets.

5   Peel and cut the sweet potato into 1-inch cubes.

6   Peel and cut the acorn squash into 1-inch cubes.

7   Once the pot of water is boiling, add the carrots, broccoli, sweet potato, and acorn squash. Cover and reduce the heat to medium.

8   Let the vegetables cook for 15 minutes, or until a fork easily pierces all of them.

9   Strain the vegetables, place them in a food processor, and pulse until smooth while gradually adding the nutritional yeast.

10 Allow to cool and serve.

NOTE: If you don't have acorn squash, you can substitute another winter squash, such as butternut or kabocha.

Squash and Greens Bowl

MONTH
9+

YIELD: 3 cups   PREP: 10 minutes
COOK: 50 minutes   TOTAL: 1 hour

great for
LUNCH

Spirulina, a funky blue-green algae, is way more than just pond scum. This biomass of cyanobacteria contains highly potent antioxidants and anti-inflammatory chemicals. Its benefits include improved brain and memory function, and its antioxidants fight free radicals. Gram for gram, it's one of the most nutritious foods on earth. Bite for baby, bite for you? See photo on page 146.

½ **cup quinoa**

½ **bunch kale (50 grams),
stems removed
and chopped**

2 **cups (340 grams)
winter squash, cut
into 1-inch cubes**

¼ **teaspoon spirulina**

1 **tablespoon nutritional yeast**

1 **tablespoon ground flaxseed**

1   Over high heat, bring 1 medium pot and 1 large pot of water to a boil.

2   Add the quinoa to the medium pot. Cover, reduce heat to low, and cook for 20 minutes, or until the quinoa feels tender and has absorbed most of the liquid.

3   Add the kale and winter squash to the large pot of boiling water. Cover, reduce heat to medium, and cook for 15 minutes.

4   Once cooked, strain the veggies and quinoa, then add them to a food processor. Pulse until smooth while gradually adding the spirulina, nutritional yeast, and ground flaxseed.

MILESTONE

At this stage, protein is working double shifts. It helps build muscles and the brain. But protein doesn't work solo. Magnesium, calcium, and choline all help develop the muscles and brain.

Ratatouille

YIELD: 4 cups   **PASSIVE:** 8 hours   **PREP:** 10 minutes
COOK: 1 hour 10 minutes   **TOTAL:** 9 hours 20 minutes

Ratatouille is an adorable Pixar movie about a rat chef *and* a traditional French dish of stewed vegetables. Tomatoes—a great way to introduce your little one to more complex, tangy flavors—are brimming with vitamin C, making them a perfect partner for iron-heavy white beans because vitamin C aids in absorbing iron. To add a pop of color and even more nutrients, this recipe includes heart-healthy kale, which has lots of vitamins A, C, and K as well as calcium. Calcium is great for strong bones of course, but it also helps the body produce melatonin for sleep, keeps heart muscles strong, and aids in nerve transmission. So say bonjour to a better night's sleep and a happy belly. Bon appétit! See photo on page 146.

2 summer zucchini (1 green and 1 yellow)

1 bunch Tuscan kale, spines removed

2 Roma tomatoes, cored

1 red bell pepper, cored and deseeded

½ cup (90 grams) dry white beans, soaked overnight

1   In a small pot over high heat, boil the tomatoes and red bell pepper for 45 to 60 minutes, until soft.

2   Strain the red veggies, then pulse them in a food processor. Set aside.

3   Drain the white beans, which have soaked in water overnight. In a small pot over high heat, boil them until soft, approximately 30 minutes.

4   Rough chop the zucchini.

5   In a medium pot over high heat, boil the zucchini pieces for 20 minutes, or until soft.

6   Mash and strain the zucchini to eliminate excess water.

7   In another medium pot, boil the kale for about 10 minutes. Strain the kale well, removing any excess water.

8   Place the zucchini and kale in a food processor and process until smooth. Set aside.

9   Transfer the white beans to a bowl and mash to your child's texture preference.

10   Layer the veggies as you like or mix them all together.

NOTES: For younger babies, process this dish to a smooth purée. Older toddlers usually can handle chunkier textures. As your child ages, here's how you can upgrade this recipe: put the ratatouille onto a pita bread, sprinkle some mozzarella on it, and toast it in the toaster oven for a special treat.

Cinnamon Blueberry Oatmeal 10+

YIELD: 2 cups **PREP: 5 minutes**
COOK: 15 minutes **TOTAL: 20 minutes**

great for BREAKFAST

Those tiny grocery-store oatmeal packages are packing a shocking amount of sugar. We're here to remind you that oatmeal is insanely easy to make, filling, healthy, and doesn't have to be a sugar bomb to taste good. Plus blueberries provide a whole lot of vitamin C.

2 cups (475 milliliters) milk, plant milk, or water

1 cup (100 grams) oats

2 to 3 tablespoons maple syrup

1 teaspoon vanilla

1 teaspoon cinnamon

½ cup (70 grams) frozen blueberries

1 to 2 tablespoons unsweetened vanilla almond milk

2 tablespoons crunchy peanut butter

Cinnamon for sprinkling

1 In a small pot over medium heat, combine the milk or water with the oats. Simmer the mixture until the oats absorb all the liquid and become smooth and creamy, 8 to 10 minutes. Make sure to stir occasionally.

2 Once the oatmeal mixture has cooked fully, add the maple syrup, vanilla, and cinnamon. Mix until well combined.

3 Remove the pot from the heat.

4 Gently fold in the frozen blueberries. They add a nice pop of flavor and cool the oatmeal so that your kiddo can enjoy it right away.

5 Divide the oatmeal among bowls.

6 Pour 1 to 2 tablespoons of almond milk over the oatmeal, add a scoop of peanut butter on the side, and top with a sprinkle of cinnamon.

NOTES: Swap the blueberries for strawberries, mango, apple, banana, or any other fruit you have on hand. Feel free to add nutmeg, rose water, or lucuma for added sweetness.

For a savory twist, add turmeric or a dash of chipotle pepper. Top it with the nut butter of your choice, dried fruit, seeds, or nuts.

154

Split Pea Dip

YIELD: 1 cup   PREP: 20 minutes
COOK: 1 hour   TOTAL: 1 hour 20 minutes

great for
LUNCH

People have been eating split peas for thousands of years. Back in 500 BCE, street vendors in Athens hawked bowls of hot pea soup. Today, the humble split pea serves as a key ingredient in many hearty dishes. Split peas have lots of fiber, protein, copper, phosphorus, B vitamins, potassium, and so much more. Best of all, the flavor is mild, which makes it a great transition food. We encourage you to let your little one dunk whatever food he or she likes into this filling and nutritious dip. Warm pita bread, soft-cooked carrots, and apples all make great options.

1 tablespoon plus 1 teaspoon olive oil

¼ medium onion, diced

1 garlic clove, minced

1 teaspoon dried basil or 2 tablespoons fresh basil, chopped

½ cup (112 grams) dried green split peas, rinsed

Zest of ½ lemon

Juice of ½ lemon

Fresh basil, for garnish

1   In a medium saucepan over medium-high heat, add 1 tablespoon olive oil and the onions. Sauté for approximately 5 minutes, until the onions become soft and translucent.

2   Add the minced garlic and basil and cook for 1 more minute.

3   Add 2½ cups (590 milliliters) of water and bring to a boil.

4   Add the split peas and reduce to a simmer.

5   Simmer, uncovered, for approximately 40 to 50 minutes. Remove from heat and allow to cool.

6   In a mixing bowl, combine the cooled, cooked split peas, lemon zest, lemon juice, and the remaining olive oil. Mix until well combined.

7   Garnish with fresh basil, if desired.

NOTE: If your baby is age 1 or older, add ⅛ teaspoon of salt, if desired.

Greens Smoothie

YIELD: 1 cup   **PREP: 5 minutes**
BLEND: 5 minutes   **TOTAL: 10 minutes**

great for SNACKS

If you break down most green smoothies, a ton of fruits typically overwhelm a little spinach or kale. This green smoothie does it differently and keeps Yumi's nutrient-dense, low-sugar mission in mind. We include cauliflower, which doesn't alter the flavor but does decrease the overall sugar level. A vitamin feast, cauliflower is high in vitamins B_5, B_6, B_9, C, and K, potassium, manganese, and fiber. Water-grown spirulina, sometimes called "vegetable plankton," contains more chlorophyll than any other food source in the world, which provides increased energy, stamina, attention, focus, and mental clarity. It also helps promote a healthy immune system, nervous system, metabolism, digestive tract, and brain. See photo on page 146.

1 cup (36 grams) packed spinach or kale

1 banana (140 grams)

½ cup (75 grams) frozen steamed cauliflower

1 kiwifruit (70 grams)

½ cup (120 milliliters) unsweetened almond milk

¼ teaspoon spirulina

1   In a blender, combine all ingredients and blend until smooth.

2   Add toppings, if desired.

NOTES: Spirulina is superconcentrated, so add only ¼ teaspoon. A little goes a long way! Feel free to substitute ¼ cup fresh or frozen mango for the kiwifruit.

Beet Burger

YIELD: eight 3-inch patties   **PREP: 15 minutes**
COOK: 45 minutes   **TOTAL: 1 hour**

It's always fun to reinvent the classics, and what's more classic than a hamburger? Our delectable plant-based burger puts a healthy spin on the all-American classic. Subtract: the sodium, red meat, and scary mystery ingredients in standard burgers. Add beets, beans, and a medley of vitamins and minerals.

You can make these burgers in the standard burger size, slider size, or bake them in a mini muffin pan for burger bites. Kids tend to love the mini version along with a fun dip, such as sour cream with chives or a Cilantro Coconut Raita (page 200). You'll love a sneaky new way to add more vegetables and nutrients into your little one's diet.

Beets offer a robust source of fiber, vitamin C, magnesium, and potassium. Black beans add hearty protein. Quinoa also is high in protein and contains all 9 essential amino acids. To top it all off, we've added onion, spices, and flaxseed meal to amp up the flavor.

continues

½ small onion
(40 grams), diced

1 tablespoon olive oil

5 to 6 small organic red
beets, peeled and shred-
ded (350 grams)

½ cup (95 grams)
cooked quinoa

½ cup (130 grams) organic
canned black beans

2 teaspoons flaxseed meal

2 teaspoons arrow-
root powder

1½ teaspoons cumin

½ teaspoon smoked paprika

¼ teaspoon ground
black pepper

¼ teaspoon pink Hima-
layan salt (if serving
to child over 1)

1 Preheat the oven to 375°F.

2 In a sauté pan over medium-high heat, add the onions and olive oil. Sauté 5 to 7 minutes, until the onions become soft and translucent.

3 In a large blender or food processor, combine the cooked onion, shredded beets, quinoa, black beans, flaxseed meal, arrowroot powder, cumin, paprika, black pepper, and salt if using.

4 Pulse the mixture—do *not* blend!—until the ingredients have mixed well but some texture remains. The mixture should resemble raw meat.

5 Transfer the mixture to a large bowl and line a baking sheet with parchment paper.

6 Using an ice cream scoop, scoop the mixture onto the baking sheet. Using a spatula, gently press the mixture flat into patties.

7 Bake the patties for 30 to 45 minutes, flipping halfway. Cooking time will vary with how thick you made the patties.

8 Serve the burgers on their own or with all the classic toppings. We suggest you load 'em up!

NOTES: Need help shredding? You could use an old-fashioned cheese grater, or you could get your hands on a salad shooter. It's a major time saver, so we love it.

When making quinoa, add 1 part quinoa to 2 parts liquid. We cook our quinoa in vegetable broth for extra flavor.

For a sturdier patty, add 1 egg in step 3 to bind the mixture better.

Sweet Po-Tater Tots

YIELD: 35 pieces   PREP: 10 minutes
COOK: 1 hour   TOTAL: 1 hour 10 minutes

great for LUNCH

In the 1950s, two brothers wanted to find a use for leftover potato scraps. They created tater tots, and we're glad they did because we love zero-waste dishes. These tots are oven baked, which makes them the perfect healthy snack for your mini. Sweet potatoes appear a lot in this cookbook for good reason. One sweet potato contains 400 percent of your kiddo's recommended daily amount of vitamin A, which keeps eyes healthy and immune system strong. Sweet potatoes get their orange color from carotenoids, which are powerful antioxidants. We blend broccoli with the sweet potatoes because they're a VIP (Very Important Plant). Broccoli contains vitamins A, K, B_6, and C, iron, and zinc. It also has lots of folate, which helps produce and maintain new cells, crucial for growing bodies.

1 sweet potato (114 grams), peeled and cubed

½ cup (45 grams) broccoli, boiled

1 pinch salt (*if serving to child over 1)

½ tablespoon garlic powder

½ cup (45 grams) oat flour

Olive oil

1   Preheat the oven to 325°F.

2   Toss sweet potatoes with olive oil (and salt*). Roast them for 40 minutes, until soft.

3   In a large bowl, combine the sweet potatoes, broccoli, and garlic powder. Using an immersion blender, whip everything together until smooth. Stir in the oat flour.

4   Line a large baking sheet with parchment paper and lightly grease it with olive oil.

5   Take a tablespoon-sized portion of the mixture and roll it into a cylinder approximately 1 inch long and ¼ inch high.

6   Bake for 8 to 10 minutes, until firm to the touch.

Independent Babes

MONTHS 12 TO 15

BADGE KEY

Immunity · Heart · Bones · Muscles · Eyes

Skin · Tummy · Sleep · Mama · Brain

Your baby has been building strength to get up, balance, and walk around. Some babies exhibit a stepping reflex when held vertically with their feet touching a flat surface. It almost looks like they're trying to take a step. It's important for your baby to get at least 30 minutes daily of adult-led physical activity to test out those sea legs.

Giving a child the freedom to choose a snack encourages independence and makes exploring the world of food fun. At this stage, you likely have introduced finger foods and your little one probably is doing some self-feeding, which fine-tunes the muscles that control a pincer grasp (or crabby claws, if you want us to get technical about it). Expect plenty of food underfoot and a messy highchair. Messy eating represents an important step in development and indicates that you're on the right—albeit filthy—track.

Red Risotto

YIELD: 3 cups　**PREP: 10 minutes**
COOK: 1 hour　**TOTAL: 1 hour 10 minutes**

great for **LUNCH**

The risotto we remember from childhood looked kind of blah and was loaded with butter and cheese. We're happy to report that risotto can be colorful, easy to make (we promise), and even healthy. Now let's talk about the ingredients. Vegetable broth adds loads of flavor, tons of nutrients, and some saltiness. Beets, a beautiful red root vegetable, are a great source of fiber, vitamin C, magnesium, and potassium. Most adults either love or hate them. Even if you don't dig them, it's important to introduce them to your kiddos. Tomatoes, a different shade of red and botanically a fruit, belong to the nightshade family. They contain lycopene, an antioxidant that reduces the risk of heart disease and cancer. Tomatoes are also high in vitamin C, potassium, folate, and vitamin K.

2 tablespoons olive oil

1 small onion (150 grams), diced

1 medium beet (80 grams), peeled and diced

2 small tomatoes, diced

1 cup (200 grams) red rice

1½ cups (355 milliliters) vegetable broth

Chopped chives, for garnish

1. In a medium sauté pan over medium heat, combine the olive oil, diced onions, and diced beets. Sauté for 5 to 7 minutes, until the onions and beets become soft.

2. Add in the diced tomatoes and sauté for an additional 2 to 3 minutes.

3. Transfer the onion, beets, and tomato to a blender and blend until smooth. Set aside.

4. In the same sauté pan over medium heat, sauté the red rice for 2 to 3 minutes, allowing it to toast slightly.

5. Add in vegetable broth, ½ cup at a time, making sure that the liquid fully absorbs before adding another ½ cup of broth.

continues

6   Once the rice has absorbed the final ½ cup of vegetable broth, add in the puréed onion, beets, and tomatoes and mix well. Keep over the heat for 2 to 3 minutes, then remove from the heat.

7   If desired, garnish with fresh chopped chives, then serve.

NOTE: Wait, didn't we tell you in Chapter 2 that rice has high concentrations of heavy metals? Yes, we did, but we also know that it's nearly impossible to avoid rice entirely. A study from Sri Lanka showed red rice had less than a fifth of the arsenic of Chinese black rice. According to the FDA, brown basmati from California, India, or Pakistan has about a third less arsenic than other brown rice.[1] Gluten-free grains such as millet or amaranth have negligible arsenic, and farro, a glutinous grain, also makes a good substitution for this recipe.

MILESTONE

At 1 year, head circumference is a good indicator of your baby's growth and development. Head-to-chest measurement is about equal at this age.

Veggie Pasta Sauce

YIELD: 5½ cups **PREP: 25 minutes**
COOK: 35 minutes **TOTAL: 1 hour**

great for
LUNCH or **DINNER**

Not all kids eat their vegetables, but almost all kids love pasta. With those two observations in mind, we created a pasta sauce that contains as many veggies as possible for those moments when your little one feels picky and ignores the broccoli you made.

In this recipe, carrots serve as a great source of fiber, vitamin A, vitamin K, and manganese. They also contain vitamins B_5, B_6, B_9, and C, iron, and potassium. Zucchini, a summer squash, has lots of potassium, fiber, vitamin A, vitamin C, and vitamin B_6. Mushrooms make a great source of omega-6 fatty acids, which help brain function, growth, and development. We use red bell peppers for their sweetness, but you can use any color that you have on hand because all of them are an amazing source of vitamin C, among other nutrients. Tomatoes, the key ingredient to any red sauce, are high in potassium and vitamins B_9, C, and K.

This sauce ticks so many boxes. Think of it as a multivitamin in liquid form.

continues

169

1 tablespoon olive oil

½ medium onion
(115 grams), finely diced

2 large carrots (375 grams),
peeled and finely diced

½ medium zucchini
(260 grams), finely diced

4 ounces mushrooms
(226 grams), finely
chopped

½ red bell pepper
(160 grams), finely diced

One 14.5-ounce (411-gram)
can organic diced
tomatoes

One 15-ounce (425-gram)
can organic tomato sauce

½ teaspoon paprika or
smoked paprika

½ teaspoon garlic powder

¼ teaspoon pink Hima-
layan salt

¼ teaspoon cracked
black pepper

1   In a large saucepan over medium-high heat, add the olive oil and onion. Sauté for 2 to 3 minutes, until the onions soften.

2   Add in the diced carrots, zucchini, mushrooms, and bell pepper. Sauté for 8 to 10 minutes, until the vegetables soften.

3   Once the vegetables are mostly soft, add in the diced tomatoes, tomato sauce, paprika, garlic powder, salt, and black pepper. Stir well to combine.

4   Simmer over low heat for 15 to 20 minutes.

5   Remove the sauce from the heat and serve immediately, or blend the sauce in a blender until smooth and serve.

NOTES: You can use almost any veggie you want in this recipe, which comes in handy when you have a fridge full of vegetables about to hit their "best by" dates. To add some protein to it, cook up a package of organic ground beef, turkey, or tofu and toss it in!

Sweet Potato Chili

YIELD: 7½ cups   PREP: 10 minutes
COOK: 45 minutes   TOTAL: 55 minutes

One-pot dishes do wonders for your health and sanity. Fun activities for a chilly, fall day: get lost in a corn maze, carve pumpkins, pick apples, and play in leaf piles. Not-so-fun activities: cook dinner. After chasing a puddle-jumping toddler all day, it's hard to gather the energy to cook a complicated meal—which is why this one-pot wonder comes in handy.

With this quick and easy recipe, you just toss a bunch of nutritious ingredients into a pot and let it stew. This chili features beans, tomatoes, and sweet potatoes. Sweet potatoes are starchy superstars and one of the few plant-based sources of vitamin B_6, which helps the brain produce serotonin and melatonin. Melatonin helps the body fall asleep and stay asleep, while serotonin stabilizes moods and promotes feelings of happiness. There's no surefire way to prevent temper tantrums, but better sleep and a healthy brain are good ways to start.

1 tablespoon olive oil

1 pound (450 grams) lean ground turkey (optional)

½ onion (100 grams), finely diced

1 garlic clove

One 15-ounce (425-gram) can navy beans, drained and rinsed

One 15-ounce (425-gram) can black beans, drained and rinsed

One 15-ounce (425-gram) can kidney beans, drained and rinsed

1 medium sweet potato (approximately 300 grams), diced

One 15-ounce (411-gram) can diced tomatoes, no salt

2 cups (500 milliliters) vegetable stock

1 tablespoon cumin

½ tablespoon coriander

½ tablespoon smoked paprika

1   If using turkey, in a large pot over high heat, add the oil and turkey. Cook until lightly browned, about 5 minutes.

2   Add the onions and sauté for 5 more minutes, until they become soft and translucent. Add the garlic and sauté for 2 to 3 more minutes.

3 Add the beans, sweet potato, tomatoes, vegetable stock, and spices. Simmer on medium for 30 to 35 minutes, until the sweet potatoes become soft and the chili thickens.

SERVING TIP: Try this recipe with the Quinoa Cornbread (see page 176).

NOTE: For a vegan version of this dish, substitute tofu for the turkey.

Mac and Cheese

YIELD: 7 cups **PREP: 15 minutes**
COOK: 50 minutes **TOTAL: 1 hour 5 minutes**

Mac and cheese is the best, but boxed macaroni has powdered milk solids or rubbery liquid "cheese" loaded with sodium and preservatives. Think outside the box for a nutritious meal that's easy and cheesy. In this recipe, nutritional yeast helps make an ooey-gooey sauce and butternut squash adds a vitamin boost that your little one will never notice. For the noodles, lentil pasta has double the protein and fiber of regular pasta. All of that means the carbs absorb slowly and steadily, which will keep (you and) your kiddo fuller longer while avoiding any blood-sugar spikes.

1 large or 1½ small fresh butternut squash (1½ pounds,
   680 grams), peeled,
   cut into 1-inch cubes

Extra virgin olive oil

1 tablespoon Earth Balance
   butter, other butter
   replacement, or butter

¾ cup (177 milliliters) milk
   or unsweetened, unfla-
   vored milk substitute

1 tablespoon oat flour or
   arrowroot powder

5 tablespoons (25 grams)
   nutritional yeast

2 teaspoons Dijon mustard

1 large clove fresh garlic
   or 2 smaller cloves

½ teaspoon onion powder

1 pound (455 grams)
   lentil pasta

Veggie Soup (page
   150, optional)

1 tablespoon fresh
   lemon juice

Salt and pepper to taste

1　Preheat the oven to 350°F and line a baking sheet with parchment paper.

2　Toss the butternut squash with extra virgin olive oil and roast for about 40 minutes, uncovered, until tender.

3　Meanwhile, prepare the "cheese" sauce. In a pot over medium heat, add the butter or butter substitute.

4　In a bowl, whisk together the milk and oat flour until any clumps dissolve. Add into the pot and whisk.

5　Whisk in the nutritional yeast, mustard, garlic, and onion powder and reduce heat to low until the mixture thickens, 5 to 7 minutes.

6　Cook the pasta according to package directions. Rinse with cool water and toss with olive oil.

7　In a blender, blend the cheese sauce with the roasted squash and some Veggie Soup if using. Add lemon juice and additional stock/milk until smooth.

8　Add salt and pepper to taste.

9　Toss cooked pasta with sauce and mix until well coated.

NOTES: To sneak in even more veggies, toss in a jar of our all-star Veggie Soup (page 150), which adds even more calcium, iron, potassium, zinc, magnesium, and lots of other vitamins. Feel free to add more nutritional yeast, to taste. You also can add ¼ cup grated Parmesan cheese for a slightly cheesier finish.

Quinoa Cornbread

YIELD: **12 pieces**   PREP: **20 minutes**
BAKE: **30 minutes**   TOTAL: **50 minutes**

Native Americans first cooked up cornbread, which long has served as a cornerstone of southern cuisine. Its popularity soared during the American Civil War because corn was cheaper than wheat. It has stood the test of time due to its versatility and unrivaled flavor.

Unfortunately, traditional cornbread has lots of carbs that can cause blood-sugar spikes. This recipe uses oat flour instead of white flour because oats are full of fiber and protein, which prevents sugars from reaching the bloodstream too quickly. Oats are also a great source of vitamin B_6, which aids in the production of serotonin and melatonin, both important for good moods and restful sleep. Quinoa contains almost twice as much protein as most other grains. Those proteins break down into a wide range of amino acids, which vitally support muscle development.

1 cup (170 grams) cooked quinoa

1 cup (150 grams) cornmeal

½ cup (45 grams) oat flour

1 cup (237 milliliters) oat milk

¼ cup (160 grams) date paste

1½ teaspoons baking powder

½ teaspoon baking soda

Cooking oil of choice, for spraying

1. Preheat the oven to 325°F.

2. Keeping the quinoa separate, combine dry ingredients into one bowl and wet ingredients into another.

3. Pour the wet ingredients slowly into the dry, mixing to combine. When fully combined, mix in the quinoa until fully incorporated.

4. Grease a 9-inch square casserole dish with cooking oil. Pour in the batter.

5. Cook on the middle rack of the oven for about 30 minutes, or until a toothpick comes out clean.

SERVING TIP: Dip this cornbread into our Sweet Potato Chili (page 172) and you'll have a hearty meal for the whole family.

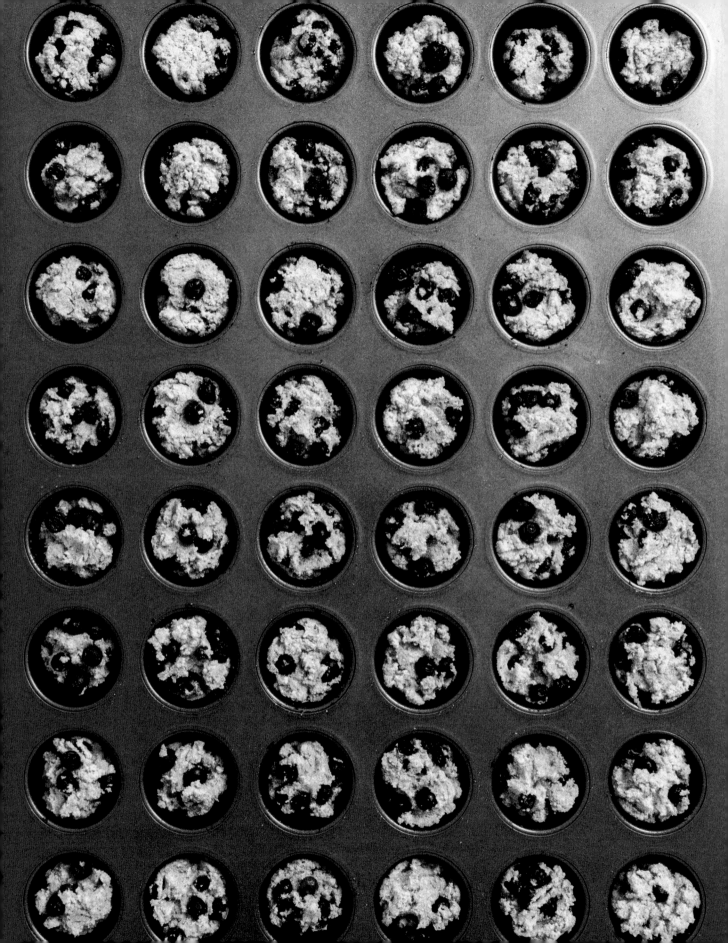

Lemon Blueberry Muffins (14+)

**YIELD: 24 mini or 12 full-sized muffins   PREP: 10 minutes
COOK: 30 to 40 minutes   TOTAL: 40 to 50 minutes**

Nothing says "grab-and-go" breakfast like a muffin. But for the most important meal of the day, the humble muffin often can fall short. Most store-bought muffins are just naked cupcakes. Full of refined white flour, oil, and sugar, they lack meaningful fiber or protein. But if you make them yourself, they can serve as the perfect morning fuel. This recipe omits refined sugar in favor of naturally sweet bananas, blueberries, and applesauce. Blueberries are packed with antioxidants, which support the heart and help decrease the likelihood of sickness and infections. Blueberries are also a great source of fiber, which promotes a healthy digestive system.

continues

WET INGREDIENTS

2 bananas (280 grams), mashed

½ cup (113 grams) vanilla or coconut yogurt

½ cup (135 grams) Apple-sauce (page 143)

½ cup unsweetened almond milk or coconut milk

1 egg

DRY INGREDIENTS

¾ cup (110 grams) oat flour

¾ cup (110 grams) coconut flour

2 teaspoons baking powder

½ teaspoon salt

MIX-INS

16 ounces fresh blueberries or 1 cup organic frozen blueberries

Zest of 1 lemon

1   Preheat the oven to 375°F.

2   In a large mixing bowl, combine the wet ingredients. Mix well.

3   Add the dry ingredients into the bowl and mix well.

4   Using a spatula, gently fold in the blueberries and lemon zest.

5   In a paper-lined or greased mini muffin tin, pour in the muffin batter until the tins are ⅔ full.

6   Bake for 22 to 24 minutes, until the tops of the mini muffins turn golden brown. If using a full-sized muffin tin, bake for 35 to 40 minutes.

7   Let cool and try not to eat them all in one sitting.

NOTE: To make these muffins gluten-free, we use a mixture of oat flour and coconut flour, but you can use whichever flours you have on hand.

Zucchini Fritters with Roasted Red Dip

YIELD: 1 cup dip, 8 fritters   PREP: 15 minutes
COOK: 35 minutes   TOTAL: 50 minutes

great for
LUNCH OR DINNER

Enjoy Christmas in July—or any other time of year—with this festive green and red plate. When snack time rolls around, it's all too easy to reach for a bag of chips, french fries, or "fruit" gummies . . . but don't! The next time you and your mini have those midday tummy rumbles, put this recipe to good use.

Zucchini is a rich source of vitamin A, magnesium, and potassium. Potassium carries oxygen to the brain, which is important for little learners. It also helps regulate blood pressure, build bones, and strengthen muscles. Our roasted red dip features bell peppers, which (surprise!) have more vitamin C than oranges. Vitamin C is just great for more than just the immune system. It also can help with insomnia and lower stress hormones. Babies constantly are learning new things and discovering new environments, so they can get just as stressed out as we do.

DIP

1 red bell pepper

8 ounces (225 grams)
   cherry tomatoes

1 garlic clove

½ tablespoon olive oil

Salt and pepper

½ tablespoon dried parsley

½ tablespoon dried basil

1 tablespoon olive oil

1   Preheat the oven to 450°F.

2   Core, seed, and halve the bell pepper. Chop the cherry tomatoes in half as well.

3   Keeping the skin on, chop the ends off the garlic clove.

4   Toss the bell pepper, cherry tomatoes, and garlic with olive oil and a sprinkle of salt and pepper.

5   Place the veggies on a baking sheet and roast them for 30 minutes, until they begin to char.

6   While the vegetables are roasting, make the zucchini fritters.

continues

181

FRITTERS

½ cup (45 grams) oat flour, finely ground

1 teaspoon baking powder

3 tablespoons olive oil

½ small onion, finely chopped

2 to 3 cloves garlic

¼ cup (20 grams) finely minced kale

1 zucchini (approximately 140 grams) shredded, squeezed, and drained of excess water

Salt and pepper to taste

½ teaspoon curry powder (optional)

Flax egg (2 tablespoons ground flaxseed + 3 tablespoons water, room temperature)

7 Sift the flour and baking powder together.

8 In a frying pan over medium-high heat, add 1 tablespoon of olive oil and the onion.

9 Sauté the onion for 3 to 5 minutes, until it begins to soften and turns translucent.

10 Add the garlic and cook for an additional 2 minutes.

11 Add the kale and cook an additional 3 to 4 minutes, until it wilts.

12 In a separate bowl, combine the zucchini, kale, onion, garlic, salt, pepper, and curry powder (if using).

13 Mix wet and dry ingredients together until fully incorporated.

14 Roll the mixture into 2-inch balls and gently press to flatten them into patties.

15 In a frying pan over medium-high heat, add the remaining 2 tablespoons of olive oil.

16 Fry the fritters in the pan for 4 minutes on each side.

17 Once the vegetables for the dip have cooled, remove the garlic skin and place the bell pepper, tomatoes, garlic, parsley, basil, and olive oil into a food processor. Mix on high until smooth.

18 Dunk the fritters into the dip.

MILESTONE

At 14 months, oral sensory-seeking behavior, or "mouthing," is normal. A form of self-soothing, it's also how babies learn and show interest in the world around them. The more they move, the more that ends up in their little mouths. Don't stress, though. Exposure to germs builds up a baby's immune system. Do be cautious of small objects, however, and redirect their attention, if possible, because babies respond better to redirection than commands.

Banana Oat Pancakes

YIELD: eight 3-inch pancakes   **PREP: 15 minutes**
COOK: 30 minutes   **TOTAL: 45 minutes**

You and your babe will want to eat these for every meal. Bananas are easy on the tummy, add natural sweetness, and are packed with fiber and potassium. Eggs are a great source of protein because they include every essential amino acid. Oats also are loaded with fiber and nutrients, making them perfect for those moments when your tummy needs a little help with digestion.

2 ripe bananas (280 grams), mashed

2 eggs

1½ cups (100 grams) oats, partially ground

1 tablespoon butter or coconut oil, for cooking

1   In a large bowl, stir the mashed bananas, eggs, and oats together until fully combined.

2   In a large frying pan over medium heat, add the butter or coconut oil.

3   Once the butter/oil has heated up, spoon or pipe the pancake batter to your desired pancake size.

4   Cook for 1 to 2 minutes on each side, until the pancakes look golden brown and feel crispy on each side.

5   Add your desired toppings and serve.

NOTES: We suggest partially grinding the oats in a food processor to make the pancakes easier for your baby to eat.

For a vegan version, use flax eggs as a substitute. For 1 flax egg, combine 1 tablespoon ground flaxseed with 3 tablespoons water. Whisk together and let the mixture sit for 15 minutes. The cooked flaxseed pancake is nice and sturdy. It doesn't fall apart, and tearing it into pieces doesn't result in messy crumbs.

185

Vegan Goldfish

YIELD: Approximately 35 crackers   **PREP: 30 minutes**
BAKE: 15 minutes   **TOTAL: 45 minutes**

great for
SNACKS

These goldfish are a golden treat. They're a perfect, worry-free, on-the-go snack with just the right amount of spice to taste-train your tot's palate, and kids love them.

1 cup (115 grams) all-purpose or whole wheat flour

5 tablespoons nutritional yeast

1 teaspoon kosher salt, divided in half

¼ teaspoon garlic powder

¼ teaspoon turmeric

¼ teaspoon paprika

6 tablespoons (95 grams) vegan butter, room temperature

1   Preheat the oven to 375°F. Line a baking sheet with parchment paper.

2   In a kitchen mixer with a paddle attachment, combine all ingredients except for ½ teaspoon of salt.

3   Blend on medium speed until the mixture begins to crumble.

4   Add 1 to 4 tablespoons cold water, 1 tablespoon at a time, until a dough forms. You shouldn't need more than 4 tablespoons of water for a good dough.

5   Remove the dough from the kitchen mixer and roll it out between two sheets of parchment paper to prevent sticking. You want the dough to be about ¼ inch thick.

6   Using a fish-shaped cookie cutter or whatever other shapes you have, cut the dough and line up the shapes on the baking sheet. Sprinkle the remaining salt on the fish.

7   Bake for approximately 15 minutes, until the bottoms of the crackers turn golden brown.

8   Let cool and serve.

NOTE: For a gluten-free option, replace the whole wheat flour with oat flour.

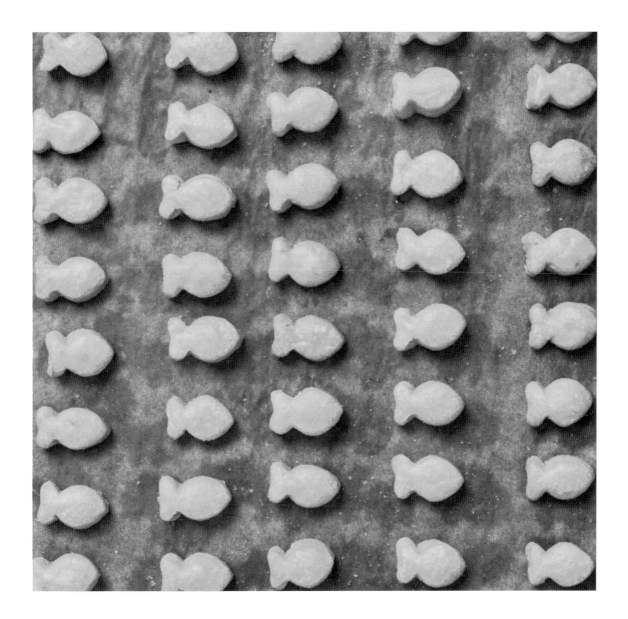

MILESTONE

You might notice that your baby shows more interest in playing with toys than other kiddos. Grabbing and picking up objects help refine their pincer grasp (which makes these goldfish the perfect snack for self-feeding). Toddlers playing side by side but together is called "parallel play." Sharing is a process, and at this stage parallel play is a wonderful opportunity to help your toddler label emotions, develop social skills, and build compassion.

187

Vegan Cheese Sauce

**YIELD: 1½ cups   PREP: 10 minutes
COOK: 30 to 40 minutes   TOTAL: 40 to 50 minutes**

Instant Pots and other programmable pressure cookers make cooking easy cheesy, and if the moon were made of cheese, we'd eat it. For vegans, people with dairy allergies, and others, nutritional yeast comes amazingly close. Sold as flakes or powder, it's a marvelous source of B vitamins and protein, especially B_{12}, which is important for brain health. Nutritional yeast is also a complete protein, which means it contains all the amino acids that a body needs but can't produce.

½ small onion or ¼ large onion, diced

2 tablespoons olive oil

¾ cup (140 grams) potatoes, peeled and diced

¾ cup (100 grams) carrots, peeled and diced

2 tablespoons lemon juice

1 teaspoon salt

¼ cup plus 2 tablespoons (30 grams) nutritional yeast

½ teaspoon garlic powder

¼ teaspoon turmeric

¼ teaspoon paprika

1   Place an Instant Pot on the SAUTÉ setting and add the onion and olive oil.

2   Sauté the onions and olive oil until the onions become soft and translucent, about 5 minutes.

3   Switch the Instant Pot to the STEW setting and add in the potatoes, carrots, ¼ cup (60 grams) water, lemon juice, and salt.

4   Set the Instant Pot timer to 30 minutes and let it work its magic.

5   Once the Instant Pot has finished cooking everything, carefully release the lid, remove the contents, and place them into a bowl.

6   Allow the cooked items to cool for 5 minutes, then transfer to a blender.

7   Add in the nutritional yeast, garlic powder, turmeric, and paprika, then blend until the cheese mixture becomes smooth and creamy. If necessary, use a spatula to scrape the sides of the blender, then blend again until smooth.

SERVING TIP: Use this dish as a dip for veggies or chips, a sauce for mac and cheese, or a topping on Taco Tuesdays. Whichever you choose, it won't disappoint.

189

Banana Bread Bites

SERVINGS: twenty 2-inch bites **PREP: 10 minutes**
PASSIVE: 1 hour **COOK: 30 minutes**
TOTAL: 1 hour 40 minutes

Make your kiddo go bananas . . . in a good way. Monkeys love bananas because they (the bananas) are bursting with flavor and nutrients. Potassium helps keep your baby hydrated and the kidneys, heart, and muscles working properly. As bananas ripen, their pectin content breaks down, making for a softer and more pliable treat that's easy for your little one to digest.

Instead of eggs, we use ground flaxseed, which is all the rage in vegan baking—and it's easy to see why. Flax "eggs" (1 tablespoon ground flaxseed, 3 tablespoons water, 15 minutes) bind ingredients together during the baking process. They also have lots of omega-3s, which aid in brain function and intelligence.

½ cup (95 grams) butternut squash, peeled, deseeded, and diced

2 teaspoons (10 grams) ground flaxseed

⅓ cup (25 grams) sorghum flour

¼ cup (30 grams) quinoa flour

1 teaspoon cinnamon

1 teaspoon lemon zest, from ½ lemon

2 medium bananas (280 grams), peeled

1 pitted date

1 teaspoon coconut oil

Avocado or vegetable oil for frying

1. Steam the butternut squash on the stovetop for 10 minutes or in the microwave for 5 minutes.

2. In a medium bowl, combine the ground flaxseed, sorghum flour, quinoa flour, cinnamon, and lemon zest.

3. Add the butternut squash, bananas, date, coconut oil, and 1 tablespoon water to a food processor. Blend until smooth. Add more water if needed.

4. Add the dry ingredients to the food processor and pulse to combine.

5. Chill the dough for 30 minutes to 1 hour.

6. Portion the dough with a small scoop, such as a melon baller, into tablespoon-sized bites.

7. In a frying pan over medium-high heat, add the avocado or vegetable oil.

8. Fry the bites for 2 to 3 minutes on each side.

MILESTONE

Even if your sleeping prince or princess has always been a great sleeper, now it's frog time. At this age, bedtime sometimes becomes more difficult, and toddlers might protest or cry after being put down to sleep. All that self-expression is hard work. Keep the same bedtime routine every night so it feels familiar and comforting, and let your kiddo have a consistent sleep-safe toy. We promise he or she won't take it to college. When tots learn new milestones, they might have a hard time sleeping. Keep an eye out for the wiggles during REM sleep.

Toddler Time

MONTHS 16 TO 18

BADGE KEY

Immunity · Heart · Bones · Muscles · Eyes

Skin · Tummy · Sleep · Mama · Brain

At 16 months, your baby is starting to understand their sense of self. As they approach their second year, the use of personal pronouns, such as "I" or "you," emerges. Yep, you're at the pearly gates of the "me do it" stage, which means your child is ready to take risks. Food risks are part of that fun! From pincer to playthings, your toddler is using their fine motor skills to make sense of the world around them. "Me do it" continues to rule as tools become part of their day-to-day. Their first real tool? A spoon. It will be messy, but let them take the risk!

During this time, you'll also notice your baby develops a more mature gait, holding their hands at their sides and moving their feet in a way that resembles walking. One part drunk baby, one part science. That's the toddler toddle.

Squash and Greens Frittata 16+

YIELD: 1 frittata PREP: 15 minutes
COOK: 20 minutes TOTAL: 35 minutes

Yumi's delicious Squash & Greens blend features oodles of nutrients, from vitamin K–packed kale to bursting-with-beta-carotene butternut squash. It's a nutrient powerhouse for the littlest person in your house. We've turned this delicious combo—not just for babies—into an amazing frittata for all. One great thing about frittatas is that you can make them ahead of time. Whip one up and keep it in your fridge for up to 48 hours. To reheat, just cut a slice, pop it in the microwave for 30 seconds, and *buon appetito*!

6 to 8 eggs

2 tablespoons whole milk or almond milk

1 teaspoon garlic powder

½ teaspoon kosher salt

½ teaspoon freshly ground black pepper

2 tablespoons olive oil

1 small onion, diced

2 cups (40 grams) fresh kale

½ cup (80 grams) fresh or frozen butternut squash

1 Preheat the oven to 400°F.

2 In a large mixing bowl, combine the eggs, milk, garlic powder, salt, and pepper. Mix well with a whisk and set aside.

3 In a medium sauté pan over medium-high heat, combine the olive oil, onion, kale, and butternut squash. Sauté for 7 to 8 minutes, until the vegetables soften.

4 Add in the egg mixture and mix into the veggies, stirring constantly for 1 minute.

5 Transfer the mixture from the pan to a casserole dish and place it in the oven.

6 Bake for approximately 10 minutes, then remove from the oven and allow to cool slightly before slicing and serving.

NOTES: You can substitute sweet potatoes for the butternut squash.

If you're a Yumi subscriber, here's a great food hack. Instead of using the kale and butternut squash listed above, add our Squash & Greens blend to the meal. Sauté the onions in olive oil and toss the contents of the Squash & Greens jar into the pan. Sauté for 30 seconds before adding the egg mixture. Instead of sautéing the veggies and the eggs for 1 minute, sauté for about 1½ minutes because the mixture will contain a bit more liquid. Then place the pan or casserole dish in the oven and bake per the directions—yum!

Tuscan White Bean and Millet Salad

YIELD: **2 cups**   PREP: **5 minutes**
COOK: **20 minutes**   TOTAL: **25 minutes**

Don't laugh, toddlers will eat salad!—especially with all the texture and taste training you've been doing. This salad begins with beans, which contain protein, magnesium, and vitamin C. They're a great source of fiber, as is millet, which contains magnesium, vitamin B_6, and iron. Tomatoes add extra vitamins A and C, and the fresh herb and lemon zest dressing will leave you feeling energized and refreshed.

SALAD

1 cup (140 grams) cooked millet

One 15-ounce can (265 grams) white beans, drained and rinsed well

2 tablespoons (8 grams) green onions (green part only), chopped

2 tablespoons (4 grams) chopped fresh basil, plus more for garnishing

2 tablespoons (3 grams) fresh parsley

½ cup (60 grams) cherry tomatoes, quartered

DRESSING

3 tablespoons olive oil

Zest of 1 lemon

Juice of 1 lemon

¼ teaspoon pink Himalayan salt

¼ teaspoon black pepper

1   In a large mixing bowl, combine the millet, white beans, green onions, basil, and parsley. Set the tomatoes aside.

2   In a small mixing bowl, whisk together the olive oil, lemon zest, lemon juice, salt, and pepper.

3   Drizzle the dressing into the large bowl and mix until the dressing evenly coats all the ingredients.

4   Gently mix in the cherry tomatoes. Garnish with basil, if desired.

5   Serve immediately or chill for eating on a hot day.

NOTE: Full of nutrients and extremely filling, this salad is great for breastfeeding mamas. For more of a protein boost, pair it with grilled chicken.

197

Sweet Potato and Millet Falafel Bites

YIELD: 24 bites   PREP: 40 minutes   COOK: 30 minutes
TOTAL: 1 hour 10 minutes   PASSIVE TIME: 24 hours

great for DINNER

We love recipes nutritious for babies but delicious for discerning foodies. This one features the chickpea, the protein-packed legume. Sweet potatoes rank low on the glycemic index, making them a smart alternative to more starchy foods. Millet, a grain rich in vitamins and minerals, traditionally is used in cereal and breads.

Coconut oil, for greasing

1 cup (180 grams) dried chickpeas, soaked for 24 hours

1 cup (230 grams) cooked sweet potato, mashed

¼ cup (40 grams) yellow onion, diced

2 teaspoons (15 grams) minced garlic (about 3 cloves)

¼ cup (6 grams) fresh parsley, chopped

¼ cup (6 grams) fresh cilantro, chopped

1 teaspoon ground cumin

½ teaspoon pink Himalayan salt

½ teaspoon ground black pepper

1 cup (140 grams) cooked millet (½ cup millet plus 1 cup vegetable broth)

1. Preheat the oven to 400°F and grease a 24-count mini muffin pan with coconut oil.

2. In a food processor, combine the chickpeas, sweet potato, onion, garlic, parsley, cilantro, cumin, salt, and pepper.

3. Blend the mixture, taking breaks to scrape the insides of the food processor. You want the mixture to combine well but still have good texture.

4. Place the blended mixture in a large bowl and, with a spatula, mix in the cooked millet.

5. Using a small ice cream scoop, create 24 balls from the falafel mixture and place in the wells of the muffin pan.

6. Bake for 30 minutes, flipping the bites halfway through. The bites may still feel soft when you flip them, but they will crisp on the edges by the end of the cooking period.

7. Once the bites are done, remove them from the oven and allow them to cool slightly before serving.

SERVING TIP: Dip the falafel bites in a yogurt and herb sauce, such as a homemade tzatziki sauce.

Cilantro Coconut Raita 16+

YIELD: 20 to 24 ounces (690 grams)   PREP: 5 minutes
WHISK: 2 minutes   TOTAL: 7 minutes

great for SNACKS

Raita, a yogurt-based condiment, originated in India. It has a cooling effect, which pairs perfectly with spicy curries and kabobs. But it also tastes delicious on tacos, grilled chicken, salmon, salads, and as a dip. To keep it dairy-free, we use coconut yogurt, which producers make by fermenting coconut flesh and adding live cultures to it, which makes it a probiotic. Because babies are born with sterile GI systems, probiotics are extremely important. Over time, kiddos build a barrier of good bacteria in their GI tracts, which prevents infection and strengthens their immune systems. Adding probiotics to their diet builds that barrier faster. Let your "little dipper" dunk some soft-cooked carrots, cooked sweet potato sticks, or naan into this dip.

One 24-ounce (680-gram) container coconut milk yogurt, plain

1 bunch cilantro, stemmed and minced

Juice of 2 lemons

1 garlic clove, grated

Salt to taste

1 Combine the yogurt, cilantro, lemon juice, grated garlic, and salt in a bowl.

2 Whisk until smooth and fully combined.

Coconut Whipped Cream 16+

YIELD: 1½ cups   PASSIVE: 6 hours
PREP: 3 minutes   WHIP: 2 minutes
TOTAL: 6 hours 5 minutes

great for
SNACKS OR DESSERT

The older your children get, the harder it becomes to avoid sugar, which reigns supreme at playdates and birthday parties. Even if you've done your best to avoid sweets at home, that toddler sugar craving will come. Coconut cream has less cholesterol, trans fat, and saturated fat than heavy cream. Both trans and saturated fats raise cholesterol, which can lead to heart disease. Coconut milk is also an excellent source of Vitamin B_{12}, which babies need for brain development and producing healthy red blood cells.

One 15-ounce can (425 grams) coconut cream
½ tablespoon maple syrup
1 teaspoon vanilla
1 pinch cream of tartar

1   Refrigerate the coconut cream for at least 6 hours.

2   Open the can and carefully remove the coconut solids, leaving any liquid in the can.

3   Using the whisk attachment on a mixer, whip the coconut solids for 1 minute, until light and fluffy.

4   Add the maple syrup, vanilla, and cream of tartar and whip for 1 more minute, until combined.

SERVING TIP: If you're struggling with "dessert," whip up this topping, the perfect alternative to store-bought whipped cream, and dollop it atop fresh berries or a cup of hot cocoa. For a savory twist, slather some on our Kabocha Squash Pie (page 223).

Date Shake

YIELD: 2 cups   **PREP: 2 minutes**
BLEND: 2 minutes   **TOTAL: 4 minutes**

great for
BREAKFAST OR **SNACKS**

No need to date other sweeteners; this date smoothie is your soul mate. Dates are nature's candy. They contain 15 minerals and 6 vitamins, including phosphorus, potassium, calcium, magnesium, and zinc. The primary ingredient in many pharmaceutical cold remedies, zinc has immune-boosting properties and helps keep germs at bay. It also helps cells grow and multiply, which is crucial for growing bodies. The potassium in bananas balances fluids in the body and maintains healthy blood pressure. Blend this scrumptious treat for your next snack date.

1 banana, peeled and frozen

4 pitted organic Medjool dates

¼ cup (60 milliliters) almond milk or milk of choice

1 tablespoon almond butter

1   Add all ingredients to a blender.

2   Blend on high for 2 minutes. Yes, 2 minutes.

NOTE: Dates can prove notoriously difficult to blend to a smooth consistency, so the longer you let the blender run, the smoother the texture will become.

Turkey Apple Meatballs

YIELD: 22 meatballs   PREP: 10 minutes
COOK: 45 minutes   TOTAL: 55 minutes

A sauce-stained high chair and floor noodles are a rite of passage for every child. But traditional can leave much to be desired. Healthy, full of flavor, and juicy, these turkey meatballs do it right. Because of their lower fat content, turkey meatballs often end up dry. We keep 'em moist with apples and carrots, which also work as binding agents. Red apples contain antioxidants that help maintain cardiovascular health and a healthy gut biome.

1 cup (100 grams) oats

½ apple (85 grams), peeled and diced

½ cup (105 grams) loosely packed shredded carrots

2 tablespoons (20 grams) diced onion

1 tablespoon oregano, fresh or dried

2 teaspoons (7 grams) minced garlic (about 3 cloves)

1 teaspoon salt

½ teaspoon paprika

¼ teaspoon black pepper

¼ teaspoon chili powder (optional)

1 pound (450 grams) ground turkey

1   Preheat the oven to 400°F. Line a baking sheet with parchment paper.

2   In a food processor, combine the oats, chopped apple, shredded carrots, diced onion, oregano, garlic, salt, paprika, black pepper, and chili powder, if using.

3   Pulse the food processor until the ingredients are finely chopped and well combined.

4   Transfer the mixture to a large mixing bowl.

5   Using a large spoon, mix the ground turkey into the oat mixture.

6   Using a spoon, scoop a golf ball–sized amount and form it into a ball. Place the meatballs on the parchment-lined baking sheet.

7   Bake for 14 to 16 minutes, until the meatballs have cooked all the way through and the outsides look golden brown.

8   Let cool and serve.

NOTE: You can swap the ground turkey for a plant-based beef substitute.

SERVING TIP: Nosh on these meatballs on their own or stack them atop some spaghetti squash noodles and smother them in our Veggie Pasta Sauce (page 169).

Future Foodies

Your 20-month-old may be able to name up to six body parts. At this age, they might have up to 50 words locked in. Those words likely include, "what's that?" and "why?" on repeat. These are two important questions for toddlers, who are trying to understand the world around them. Repetition helps them gain and cement new knowledge. This is a great time to talk to your future foodie about new foods.

Give them as much "what" and "why" as you can. It pays off. That doesn't mean entirely smooth sailing. You've worked hard to avoid a picky eater, so at 21 months, what gives? When mealtime interrupts playtime, some toddlers have a hard time focusing. Your baby may stop eating because they are bored—rather than full—so some encouragement could be necessary. A good way to make sure they are getting what they need is to eat at the same time as your child, and to eat the same thing. If that's not possible, then at least try to sit with them while they eat, as this will stop them wanting to play up to get your attention.

Now that they are on the go, you want to keep them as healthy as possible with immunity-boosting foods.

Baby Dragon Fruit Smoothie 19+

YIELD: 5 cups (1.2 liters)   **PREP: 5 minutes**
BLEND: 5 minutes   **TOTAL: 10 minutes**

Smoothies can be controversial for little ones because usually they're loaded with fruit sugars. Fructose is natural, but too much is too much—especially when displacing other nutrients. Cauliflower, our secret to keeping smoothie sugar levels low, cuts the sweetness of the fruit while adding a thick and creamy texture. Cauliflower is also high in fiber, vitamins B_5, B_6, B_9, C, and K, potassium, and manganese. You can chop it up ahead of time, steam it, freeze it, and then toss it into any smoothie.

Dragon fruit, also naturally low in sugar but rich in antioxidants, B vitamins, and vitamin C, adds gorgeous color to this drink. Bananas add fiber and potassium, pineapple provides vitamin C and manganese, and raspberries supply antioxidants, vitamin C, manganese, copper, and fiber. Baobab powder, which comes from Africa's "tree of life," is a rich source of vitamin C, promotes regular immune function, and contributes to healthy skin.

1 ripe banana (140 grams)

One 12-ounce packet (340 grams) frozen pitaya (dragon fruit)

½ cup (105 grams) frozen steamed cauliflower

½ cup (118 milliliters) almond milk

½ cup (170 grams) raspberries

½ cup (230 grams) pineapple

1 teaspoon (4 grams) baobab powder

1   In a large blender, combine all ingredients and blend until well combined.

2   Add toppings, if desired.

NOTES: If your baby is sensitive to nut milks, use any other plant milk of choice, such as coconut, hemp, or oat milk. To "adult it up," additional options include chopped fruit, almond butter, shredded coconut, chia seeds, and flaxseed.

SERVING TIP: Your toddler can drink this smoothie from a cup or spoon it from a bowl.

Turmeric Overnight Oats with Mango Compote

YIELD: 4 cups (360 grams)   PREP: 15 minutes
PASSIVE: 8 hours   TOTAL: 8 hours 15 minutes

Oats, a protein powerhouse, are one of the few sources of avenanthramides, which help lower blood pressure. They have anti-inflammatory and anti-itching effects, which is why oatmeal baths are great if your toddler has an itchy rash or dry skin. The beta-glucan in oats lowers cholesterol, keeps you full, and encourages the growth of good bacteria in your digestive system. Turmeric contains curcumin, an anti-inflammatory and antioxidant that improves the lining of your blood vessels, which helps to regulate blood pressure and clotting.

OATMEAL

2 cups (200 grams) oats

2 cups (473 milliliters) plant milk or water

1 tablespoon (22 grams) lucuma

3 tablespoons (125 grams) date paste

½ teaspoon vanilla extract

½ teaspoon turmeric

1 teaspoon (60 grams) chia seeds (optional)

1 pinch salt

MANGO COMPOTE

1 fresh mango, diced into ½-inch cubes, or 8 ounces frozen mango

2 tablespoons maple syrup

½ teaspoon vanilla

1   In a large bowl, mix all the oatmeal ingredients until well combined.

2   Divide the mixture evenly into four jars.

3   For the compote, if using frozen mango, cook the pieces over medium-high heat until soft. Add maple syrup and vanilla.

4   Cook for 10 minutes, stirring often, as the mixture bubbles and thickens.

5   Remove the compote from the heat and allow it to cool. Divide it among the four jars, atop the oat mixture. Add any additional desired toppings, such as chopped walnuts.

6   Seal the jars with their lids and refrigerate overnight.

Overnight Oats with Rose and Berry Compote 19+ MONTH

YIELD: 4 cups (360 grams)   **PREP: 5 minutes**
COOK: 15 minutes   **PASSIVE: 8 hours**   **TOTAL: 8 hours 20 minutes**

great for BREAKFAST

Ancient Persians first explored the culinary uses of rose water, using it to season and infuse their foods. Today it's making a comeback. Rose water is rich in phenolics, which are anti-inflammatory. It also is loaded with vitamins A, B, C, and E. Raspberries and blackberries brim with antioxidants, but what does that mean? Oxygen causes silver to tarnish and iron to rust. On a molecular level, it does the same thing inside our bodies. Antioxidants combat the free radicals that result from that oxidation. So fight those free radicals with a flowery feast.

OATMEAL

2½ cups (250 grams) oats

1 tablespoon lucuma

2 cups (480 grams) oat milk, plain, unsweetened

3 tablespoons (125 grams) date paste

½ teaspoon vanilla extract

½ teaspoon cinnamon

1 teaspoon chia seeds

1 pinch salt

ROSE AND BERRY COMPOTE

⅓ cup (70 grams) raspberries

⅓ cup (55 grams) blackberries

1 drop rose water

1 tablespoon maple syrup

⅛ teaspoon vanilla extract

1   First make the oatmeal. In a large bowl, mix all the oatmeal ingredients together until well combined.

2   Divide the mixture evenly among four jars.

3   Next make the compote. In a pot over medium heat, add the berries, rose water, maple syrup, and vanilla extract.

4   Cook for 10 minutes and stir often as the mixture bubbles and thickens.

5   Remove the compote from the heat and allow it to cool. Divide it among the four jars, atop the oat mixture.

6   Seal the jars with their lids and refrigerate overnight.

NOTE: Just 1 drop of rose water, no more. It's very strong!

215

Sweet Potato Skins

YIELD: 8 sweet potato skins   **PREP: 5 minutes**
COOK: 1 hour 10 minutes   **TOTAL: 1 hour 15 minutes**

For days that require a thick skin, make a snack that has one, too. This snack ticks all the craving boxes: crunchy, sweet, savory, salty. Sweet potatoes have lots of vitamin A, which supports organ growth and development, but they fall lower on the glycemic index than other potatoes, which makes them less likely to spike blood sugar. Anything potatoes can do, sweet potats can do better. Their high beta-carotene content gives sweet potatoes their orange hue. That nutrient not only strengthens eyesight, but it also boosts your little one's immune system, helping to protect against severe asthma attacks.

4 small sweet potatoes
¼ cup (22 grams) broc-coli, minced, boiled, and drained
Salt and pepper to taste
Olive oil for cooking

NOTE: Some babies who *really* love veggies with a lot of beta-carotene can develop an orange tint to their skin. If this happens, don't panic—it's not harmful at all. Your baby's body uses only as much beta-carotene as it needs, depositing the rest in the skin. As your baby explores other foods, the orange hue will dissipate slowly.

1   Preheat the oven to 400°F. Line a large baking sheet with parchment paper or a silicone baking mat.

2   Pierce each sweet potato a few times and bake for 40 to 50 minutes, until soft.

3   Allow the potatoes to cool slightly. Slice potatoes in half lengthwise.

4   Reduce the oven temperature to 375°F.

5   Scoop out the sweet potato flesh, leaving a thin layer of sweet potato inside. Add the flesh to a medium bowl.

6   Place the skins back onto the baking sheet, hollow side up, drizzle with olive oil, and bake for 10 minutes.

7   While the skins are baking, mash the sweet potato flesh until smooth and creamy. Stir in the minced broccoli.

8   Once the skins have finished baking, scoop the sweet potato and broccoli mixture back into the skins.

9   Top with chopped chives, shredded cheese, sour cream, diced avocado, or other toppings of your choice.

Quesadillas

**YIELD: 8 quesadillas   PREP: 15 minutes
PASSIVE: 1 hour   COOKING: 40 minutes
TOTAL: 1 hour 55 minutes**

A traditional quesadilla can deliver all the fat and sodium in a daily allowance and then some. To make this a well-balanced meal, we added beans, tomatoes, and a nutritional yeast "cheese" sauce.

Beans provide lots of powerful plant protein, essential for your little one's growth and development. Protein repairs tissue, balances body fluids, clots blood, contracts muscles, and aids in digestion. Nutritional yeast, one of the few plant-based sources of vitamin B_6, boosts serotonin and norepinephrine, helping kiddos feel happier and less stressed.

We encourage you to make your own corn tortillas or buy organic ones. Corn tortillas are gluten-free and have fewer calories, sodium, and carbs.

TORTILLAS

½ teaspoon sea salt

2 cups (300 grams) Bob's Red Mill Corn Flour

FILLING

One 15-ounce can (425 grams) white beans, drained

1 garlic clove, minced

¼ cup (25 grams) nutritional yeast

1 teaspoon ground cumin

¾ cup (135 grams) diced tomatoes

½ cup (70 grams) black beans, cooked and drained

1   First make the tortillas. Mix the salt into the corn flour.

2   Slowly pour 1½ to 2 cups (350 to 475 grams) hot water into the flour mixture to get a good consistency. It should feel firm and springy to the touch, not dry or sticky. Let it rest for about 1 hour, covered with a damp towel.

3   Preheat a griddle or frying pan. Divide the dough into 2-inch balls. Press the dough between 2 pieces of wax paper, or flatten in a tortilla press, into 6-inch circles.

4   Cook the tortilla on one side for about 1 minute, then flip it over and heat for 1 more minute.

5   Next make the filling. In a food processor, blend the white beans and garlic together. Add in the nutritional yeast and cumin. Process on high until fully incorporated.

6   Transfer the bean blend to a large bowl. Stir the tomatoes and black beans into the blended bean mixture.

7   Spread the mixture between two tortillas.

NOTE: If you don't have time to make homemade tortillas, we *tortilla* get it. We recommend these healthy, ready-to-eat options: Tia Lupita, La Tortilla Factory, and Masienda.

SERVING TIP: These quesadillas are delicious topped with guacamole, salsa, or plain Greek yogurt.

Plantain Empanadas

YIELD: 20 empanadas   PREP: 25 minutes
COOK: 2 hours   TOTAL: 2 hours 25 minutes

The plantain, banana's tough and bitter cousin, tastes starchier and earthier than a banana. People call them "cooking bananas" because they're much more palatable when cooked, and you can prepare them like potatoes: baked, boiled, fried, or mashed. Packed with vitamins A, B, and C, they strengthen babies' eyesight, skin, immune system, and digestive system.

Black beans are a staple around the world but are especially popular in their native Central and South America. They're versatile, nutritious, and affordable, making them a new mama's best friend. They also are brimming with iron and zinc, two essential nutrients that babies often lack. Breast milk contains little iron, so by 6 months babies need more of that mighty metal. Eating black beans with foods high in vitamin C, such as kale and plantains, boosts baby's ability to absorb all the iron.

4 large plantains, very ripe

1½ tablespoons olive oil, plus more for brushing and cooking

¼ cup (12 grams) kale, shredded and minced

2 cloves fresh garlic

1 cup (170 grams) cooked black beans

1   In a medium pot over high heat, boil the plantains in their skins for 20 to 25 minutes.

2   Remove the skins, transfer the plantains to a bowl, add in ½ tablespoon olive oil, and mash.

3   In a medium pan over medium-high heat, sauté the kale and garlic in 1 tablespoon olive oil, until wilted, about 2 minutes.

4   Using a food processor or a stick blender and a medium bowl, purée the beans. Remove any excess liquid. Stir in cooked kale and garlic.

5   Brush the insides of two pieces of parchment paper with olive oil. Line a tortilla press with them.

continues

6   Using the tortilla press, flatten 2 tablespoons of mashed plantains into a patty and transfer plantain patty onto a plate.

7   Place about 1 teaspoon of black bean mixture in the middle of the patty.

8   Gently fold the edges over the bean mixture to form an empanada. Press edges together to close.

9   Repeat until you have created all your raw empanadas.

10 In a large frying pan over medium heat, add olive oil and fry the empanadas for 4 minutes on each side.

11 Serve with guacamole.

NOTE: If you don't have a tortilla press, you can press the plantains into shape, still between two sheets of oil-brushed parchment paper, with a pie plate or other heavy round container or pot.

Kabocha Squash Pie

YIELD: One 9-inch pie　**PASSIVE: 8 hours**
PREP: 15 minutes　**BAKE: 45 minutes**
TOTAL: 9 hours

great for
DINNER or DESSERT

Kabocha squash, a Yumi favorite, is a low-carb, fibrous food packed with beta-carotene, which improves blood, skin, and hair health. It's also a good source of iron, vitamin C, and B vitamins. If it's not in season, you can substitute butternut squash. We use almond milk, maple syrup, eggs, and spices to create a creamy filling, and the perfectly crunchy cashew-based crust tastes subtly sweet. Pepitas, pistachios, and shaved tigernuts add extra texture. To make the recipe easier to chew for younger tots, swap the cashew crust for a regular organic pie crust. No matter how you make it, you can enjoy a nice slice of pie without the sugar overload.

CRUST

1½ cups (335 grams) cashews, soaked overnight)
½ cup (50 grams) oats
5 dates (40 grams)
¼ cup (80 milliliters) maple syrup
¼ teaspoon salt

1. First make the crust. Preheat the oven to 375°F.

2. Drain the liquid from the soaked cashews.

3. In a food processor, add all the crust ingredients and blend until the cashew pieces are chopped well and the mixture is cohesive.

4. Into a pie pan, evenly spread the crust mixture.

5. Bake for approximately 20 minutes, until the edges of the crust turn golden brown.

6. Next make the filling. In a food processor, place all the filling ingredients and blend on low until completely smooth.

continues

223

FILLING

2 cups (400 grams) roasted kabocha squash

½ cup (105 milliliters) unsweetened vanilla almond milk

¼ cup (80 milliliters) maple syrup

2 eggs (100 milliliters)

2 teaspoons cinnamon

1 teaspoon vanilla

½ teaspoon ginger

½ teaspoon salt

TOPPING

¼ cup (30 grams) pepitas (raw pumpkin seeds)

¼ cup (30 grams) pistachios

1 teaspoon maple syrup

1 tablespoon tigernuts, grated

7 Fill the baked pie crust with the kabocha squash filling and place it back in the oven for approximately 25 minutes.

8 Remove from the oven and allow to cool.

9 For the topping, in a small bowl, combine the pepitas, pistachios, and maple syrup.

10 In a small frying pan over low heat, cook the topping mixture for 2 to 3 minutes, then remove from heat.

11 Spread the topping mixture along the perimeter of the pie and top it with tigernut shavings.

12 Serve immediately or store in the fridge for up to 3 days.

SERVING TIP: To make this pie taste a little more like dessert, add a dollop of fresh Coconut Whipped Cream (page 202) and a sprinkle of cinnamon.

Lentil Chili Sliders

YIELD: 4 cups   **PREP: 10 minutes**
COOK: 35 minutes   **TOTAL: 45 minutes**

Here's another one-pot wonder to make your life easier. Slather the chili inside a slider bun, and you have a slightly messy but completely delicious dinner for the whole family. Lentils are an amazing source of fiber, copper, iron, B vitamins, and more. Onions add phytochemicals and vitamin C, which help boost the immune system. Bell pepper, tomatoes, and spinach add an extra nutrient boost, while cumin, lucuma, paprika, and black pepper add warmth and flavor.

1 cup (210 grams) green lentils, rinsed

2 cups (500 grams) vegetable broth

½ onion (60 grams), diced

½ red bell pepper (85 grams), diced

1 teaspoon (4 grams) garlic, minced

1 tablespoon olive oil

1 cup (70 grams) frozen spinach or 3 cups fresh spinach

3 tablespoons Worcestershire sauce or vegan substitute

One 15-ounce can (435 grams) tomato sauce (no salt added)

1 teaspoon cumin

1 teaspoon lucuma

½ teaspoon paprika

¼ teaspoon black pepper

Slider buns, if desired

1   In a small pot, combine the green lentils and vegetable broth. Bring to a boil, then reduce heat to a simmer.

2   Simmer for approximately 20 minutes, or until the lentils have absorbed all the liquid and have become tender. Remove from heat.

3   In a large frying pan, combine the onion, red bell pepper, garlic, and olive oil. Sauté for 4 to 5 minutes, until onions and bell pepper soften.

4   Add in the spinach and sauté for another 2 to 3 minutes.

5   Add in the Worcestershire sauce and mix well with the veggies. Add in the tomato sauce and lentils.

6   Finally, mix in the cumin, lucuma, paprika, and black pepper. Simmer for approximately 5 more minutes.

7   Serve immediately on its own or in the slider buns of your choice.

SERVING TIP: Toast the slider buns first to keep them from becoming soggy.

Sweet Potato Latkes

YIELD: twelve 3-inch latkes   PREP: 40 minutes
BAKE: 55 minutes   TOTAL: 1 hour 35 minutes

Latkes, a golden, crispy classic, often can lead to a bloated tummy. We love reinventing the classics with healthier ingredients, which is why we use baked sweet potatoes for this recipe. Yes, crispy baked latkes are possible. Sweet potatoes rank low on the glycemic index and are packed with potassium, beta-carotene, vitamin C, vitamin B_6, and other vitamins and minerals. Oats add extra fiber, which will leave you feeling fuller longer. Make these into bite-sized latkes for your little one or for the whole family. They keep well in the fridge, making them a great option for a snack made ahead of time. L'chaim!

**2 cups (660 grams) shred-
    ded sweet potato**

½ cup (50 grams) oats

1 egg (60 grams)

2 tablespoons almond flour

**1 tablespoon dried
    minced onion**

1 garlic clove, chopped

½ teaspoon cumin

¾ teaspoon salt

½ teaspoon black pepper

2 tablespoons olive oil

1   In a large bowl, combine the shredded sweet potato and oats. Let them sit for 30 minutes, which allows the oats to soak up moisture from the shredded sweet potato.

2   Add the egg, almond flour, minced onion, garlic, cumin, salt, and pepper. Mix until well combined.

3   Preheat the oven to 375°F and line a baking sheet with parchment paper.

4   Using your hands, form small patties with the sweet potato mixture. Lightly brush each side of the latke with olive oil.

5   Carefully place the patties onto the parchment paper.

6   Bake the latkes for approximately 15 minutes.

7   Flip them and put them back in the oven for another 7 to 8 minutes, until crispy.

SERVING TIP: At a party, pair these with creamy horseradish or herbed feta dip. The possibilities are endless.

229

Beanballs

YIELD: 20 beanballs   PREP: 15 minutes
PASSIVE: 1 hour   COOK: 1 hour
TOTAL: 2 hours 15 minutes

With whole ingredients and no curveballs, these plant-based meatballs are packed with flavor. Lentils contain lots of fiber, zinc, calcium, folate, and iron. Iron supports a baby's psychological development, social development, and ability to focus. In addition to providing a rich savory taste, mushrooms add a whole host of nutrients. A prebiotic, they help build good bacteria in your baby's digestive tract. They are also rich in zinc, potassium, B vitamins, and copper. Copper helps the body absorb iron, keeping blood vessels, nerves, immune system, and bones healthy. Roll these babies up, and your baby will be ready to roll!

1 cup (250 grams) lentils, rinsed and picked over

1½ cups (350 milliliters) vegetable broth

2 tablespoons olive oil

1 small onion, finely diced

2 cloves garlic

1½ teaspoons apple cider vinegar

13 ounces (370 grams) cremini mushrooms

1 teaspoon fresh thyme leaves

Salt and pepper to taste

3 tablespoons rolled oats

1 flax egg (1 tablespoon ground flaxseed in 3 tablespoons water for 15 minutes)

⅓ cup (50 grams) oat flour

1   In a medium saucepan over medium-high heat, combine the rinsed lentils and vegetable broth and bring to a boil. Reduce the heat to a low simmer.

2   Simmer for 20 to 30 minutes, until the lentils soften. Add more vegetable broth if needed.

3   Meanwhile, in a medium skillet over medium heat, add 1 tablespoon olive oil and the onions and sauté until translucent, 5 to 7 minutes. Add the garlic and apple cider vinegar and cook for another 2 minutes, until the vinegar absorbs.

4   Add in the mushrooms, thyme leaves, and pepper. Cook until the mushrooms slightly soften and begin to brown, about 10 minutes. Add salt.

5   Remove from heat and transfer to a large bowl. Stir in the rolled oats, cooked lentils, and flax egg. Mix in the oat flour until well combined.

6   Roll the mixture into golf ball–sized balls and refrigerate the beanballs for 45 minutes to 1 hour.

7   In a skillet over medium heat, add 1 tablespoon olive oil and fry the meatballs for 4 to 5 minutes, until golden brown. Roll the beanballs around each minute to ensure they cook evenly.

Hemp Seed Ranch Dip

YIELD: 4 cups **PREP: 5 minutes**
BLEND: 5 minutes **TOTAL: 10 minutes**

Home, home on the ranch. Store-bought ranch dressing often contains high amounts of unsaturated fat, which raises cholesterol levels and increases the risk of heart disease. But sometimes ranch dressing is the only way to get your kiddo to eat those veggies, which is where our Hemp Seed Ranch Dip comes into play.

One of the fastest-growing plants on earth, hemp can be made into paper, rope, clothing, "plastic," paint, and of course food. Hemp seeds contain high levels of protein, vitamin E, phosphorus, potassium, sodium, magnesium, sulfur, calcium, iron, and zinc. They also have omega fatty acids that fight inflammation, protect the heart, and strengthen the immune system. (Just in case you're worried, no, they don't contain any mind-altering chemicals.)

4 cups (600 grams) hemp seeds
juice of 2 lemons
1 to 2 cloves fresh garlic
1 ounce (28 grams) chives
1 tablespoon dried dill weed
1 teaspoon onion powder
1 teaspoon garlic powder
Salt and pepper to taste

In a blender, combine all ingredients and blend on high, adding 1 to 2 cups (235 to 470 grams) water until you achieve a thick, smooth sauce.

SERVING TIP: We recommend soft-cooking some carrots, sweet potato sticks, broccoli, or cauliflower and letting your toddler submerge them into this dip.

Beet Chips (19+)

YIELD: 1 cup   PREP: 45 minutes
BAKE: 1 hour   TOTAL: 1 hour 45 minutes

We hate throwing away rotten vegetables. Food-waste guilt is real. An easy way to prevent veggies from going to waste is to turn them into chips, which are surprisingly simple to make. Just peel the vegetables, slice them using a mandoline, dry them, and pop them into the oven.

3 to 5 small beets
1 teaspoon kosher salt
¼ teaspoon onion powder
⅛ teaspoon garlic powder

1   Peel the beets and slice them thinly on a mandoline.

2   Lay out a couple of paper towels and spread the beet slices on them, making sure they don't overlap.

3   Sprinkle the beets with salt and allow them to rest on the paper towels for about 30 minutes.

4   Preheat the oven to 250°F.

5   Using a second layer of paper towels, dab the excess moisture from the beets.

6   Line a baking sheet with parchment paper and transfer the beet slices to the baking sheet.

7   Sprinkle the beet slices with onion powder, garlic powder, or your seasonings of choice.

8   Bake for 1 to 1½ hours, depending on how thinly you sliced the beets and how crispy you like your chips.

9   Allow the chips to cool and serve.

NOTES: The parchment paper is crucial for crisping up the chips, so no substitutions there. Also, you can use pretty much any vegetable in your kitchen with this recipe. Get creative!

Spiced Molasses Cookies

YIELD: 30 mini cookies   **PREP: 20 minutes**
BAKE: 10 minutes   **TOTAL: 30 minutes**

We're not monsters. We just want to keep your kiddo from becoming one. Memories of cookies suffuse our childhoods. To this day, no aroma conjures nostalgia quite like a warm kitchen after baking holiday cookies. Now that we're older, our metabolisms and our blood sugar levels can't handle gobs of cookie dough and sprinkles. As we make our own holiday cookie memories with our children, it's important to teach them that delicious can mean healthy. We encourage you to make this recipe with your little one. Those little fingers will love helping you mix, roll, and shape. Kick up that holiday spirit with some festive sprinkles or a light touch of confectioners' sugar glaze.

1¼ cup (175 grams) whole wheat flour

1 teaspoon baking powder

1 teaspoon ginger

½ teaspoon cinnamon

¼ teaspoon nutmeg

¼ teaspoon ground cloves

¼ teaspoon kosher salt

2 tablespoons butter, room temperature

1 tablespoon natural sweetener, such as Stevia

1 egg (60 grams), room temperature

1 teaspoon vanilla extract

¼ cup (60 milliliters) molasses

Confectioners' sugar, for dusting

1. Sift together the whole wheat flour, baking powder, ginger, cinnamon, nutmeg, ground cloves, and kosher salt. Set aside.

2. In a kitchen mixer with a paddle attachment, cream the butter and sweetener together at high speed for 2 to 3 minutes.

3. At medium speed, beat the egg and vanilla extract into the mixture until just combined. Scrape down the sides of the bowl.

4. Alternate adding half of the dry ingredients with half of the molasses until it all completely incorporates.

5. Form the dough into a ball, wrap it in plastic wrap, and refrigerate for 1 hour.

6. Preheat the oven to 375°F.

7. Remove the dough ball from the fridge, remove the plastic wrap, and place the dough between two sheets of parchment paper.

8. Roll out the dough to a ¼-inch thickness.

9   Carefully remove the top piece of parchment paper and, using a cookie cutter, cut the dough into your desired shapes.

10   Place the cookie shapes on an ungreased baking sheet and top with a light sprinkle of sugar.

11   Bake for 7 to 8 minutes, until the bottom of the cookie develops a crust.

12   Allow to cool and dust with more sugar to taste.

237

Raspberry Coconut Shaved Ice

YIELD: 6 cups (2,040 grams)   **BLEND: 5 minutes**
PASSIVE: 2 hours   **PREP: 15 minutes**
TOTAL: 2 hours 20 minutes

After a long day of sunscreen, floaties, and doggy paddling, it's hard to resist an ice-cold treat. Most store-bought frozen treats usually are swimming in unhealthy syrups loaded with sugar, artificial flavors, and dyes. But you can chill out with this recipe, knowing that your little one is getting essential nutrients in a delectable dessert. The star of this cool confection, raspberries are loaded with antioxidants, vitamin C, and fiber. When introduced to solids, babies often develop constipation, which makes fiber an important part of their diet. It also increases feelings of fullness, lowers cholesterol, and prevents heart disease and diabetes—all for the win! Coconut milk, an excellent source of niacin, iron, and copper, is rich in lauric acid, which gives breast milk its amazing ability to help fight infections.

4 pints (1 kilogram) fresh raspberries
Two 13.5-ounce cans (398 milliliters) coconut milk
¼ cup (80 milliliters) maple syrup
1 dash pink Himalayan salt
1 teaspoon vanilla extract

1   In a blender, add the raspberries and blend until smooth.

2   Run the puréed raspberries through a sieve to remove the seeds. If you like a little more texture, skip this step.

3   If straining, put the strained raspberry purée back into the blender. Add in the coconut milk, maple syrup, salt, and vanilla extract.

4   Blend for approximately 30 seconds, then transfer the mixture to a deep baking sheet or storage container.

5   Freeze the mixture for 1 to 2 hours, until completely frozen.

6   Remove the container from the freezer and let it sit at room temperature for 5 to 10 minutes, until you're able to scrape off layers to make shaved ice.

Acknowledgments

Our friend and advisor Josette Sheeran, former head of the UN World Food Programme, once said "Food is one issue that cannot be solved person by person. We have to stand together." Like our collective mission to raise a healthier generation, this book also stands on the shoulders of many.

Or, in parenting parlance, it takes a village.

Thank you to Angela Sutherland, without whom this book and Yumi wouldn't exist. To her children for inspiring the entire idea; as is said, children are our greatest teachers. To the entire Yumi team for putting up with us as we wrote this book and missed other deadlines. Dr. Anthony Porto for believing in our mission and putting words to page that say so. Dr. Michael Goran, Dr. Dina DiMaggio, and Josette Sheeran for inspiring us with your research and work in childhood development, public policy, and nutrition.

To the amazing team at Park & Fine Literary, including our agents Anna Petkovich and John Mass, who fielded texts and calls and emails ad infinitum (and Eric Nelson for bringing us all together). Ann Treistman, who believed in this book, even when we pitched it from a laundry room. Our editor, James Jayo, who works magic with every stroke of the key. Thomas Mastorakas for his brilliance and straight-shooting. To Tia Langley for being an absolute recipe-testing unicorn. Alexandra Krymsky for her research and supernatural organizational skills, Maya Hull for photo assisting and living inside Ari's kitchen, and Tiffanee Wilcox for simply living inside our brains.

To our many teachers and mentors along the way, Jane Perlez and Raymond Bonner for inspiring Evelyn to be a writer; Antoinette Nolan, who taught Ari to be OK with a redline; and Steve Schioldager, who taught her when to ignore it. To Angela's mother, Julie Brown, who passed down her entrepreneurial motor. To David Hornik, Dr. Andrew Firlik, Adam Miller, Ido Leffler, Jordan Gaspar, and Dan Rosensweig for your Yoda-like guidance and to Anjula Acharia, Desiree Gruber, Anita Chatterjee, Chris and Sarah Dawson, and Bryan Meehan for being our biggest, pom-pom wielding cheerleaders.

To our husbands, Daniel Gruenberg and Eli Thomas, whose extreme patience and support deserve to be treasured. To Ari's daughter Basil, who is already quick to correct grammar and already has applied to be the editor of our second book.

Notes

INTRODUCTION

1. JH Gilmore, RK Santelli, and W Gao, "Imaging Structural and Functional Brain Development in Early Childhood," *Nature Reviews Neuroscience* 19, no. 3 (February 16, 2018): 123–137, https://doi.org/10.1038/nrn.2018.1.

2. Copenhagen Consensus 2012, www.copenhagenconsensus.com/sites/default/files/outcome_document_updated_1105.pdp. Bjørn Lomborg, *How to Spend $75 Billion to Make the World a Better Place*, 2nd ed., Copenhagen Consensus Center, 2014.

CHAPTER 1

1. AA Geraghty, KL Lindsay, G Alberdi, FM McAuliffe, and ER Gibney, "Nutrition During Pregnancy Impacts Offspring's Epigenetic Status—Evidence from Human and Animal Studies," *Nutrition and Metabolic Insights* 8, no. 1 (February 16, 2016): 41–47, https://doi.org/10.4137/NMI.S29527.

2. R Gabbianelli, L Bordoni, S Morano, J Calleja-Agius, and JD Lalor, "Nutri-Epigenetics and Gut Microbiota: How Birth Care, Bonding and Breastfeeding Can Influence and Be Influenced?" *International Journal of Molecular Sciences* 21, no. 14 (July 16, 2020): 5032, https://doi.org/10.3390/ijms21145032.

3. MVE Veenendaal, RC Painter, SR de Rooij, PMM Bossuyt, JAM van der Post, PD Gluckman, MA Hanson, and TJ Roseboom, "Transgenerational Effects of Prenatal Exposure to the 1944–45 Dutch Famine," *BJOG* 120, no. 5 (January 24, 2013): 548–554, https://doi.org/10.1111/1471-0528.12136.

4. F Robin-Champigneul, "Jeanne Calment's Unique 122-Year Life Span: Facts and Factors; Longevity History in Her Genealogical Tree," *Rejuvenation Research* 23, no. 1 (February 17, 2020): 19–47, https://doi.org/10.1089/rej.2019.2298.

5. P Lally, C Jaarsveld, H Potts, and J Wardle. "How Are Habits Formed: Modelling Habit Formation in the Real World," *European Journal of Social Psychology* 40, no. 6 (October 2010): 998–1009, https://doi.org/10.1002/ejsp.674.

6. M Lenoir, F Serre, L Cantin, and SH Ahmed, "Intense Sweetness Surpasses Cocaine Reward," *PLoS ONE* 2, no. 8 (August 1, 2007): e698, https://doi.org/10.1371/journal.pone.0000698.

7. R Martorell, "Improved Nutrition in the First 1000 Days and Adult Human Capital and Health," *American Journal of Human Biology* 29, no. 2 (March 2017): e22952, 10.1002/ajhb.22952. https://doi.org/10.1002/ajhb.22952.

8. World Health Organization, "WHO Guidance Helps Detect Iron Deficiency and Protect Health Development," news release, April 20, 2020, https://www.who.int/news/item/20-04-2020-who-guidance-helps-detect-iron-deficiency-and-protect-brain-development#:~:text=Iron%20deficiency%20is%20the%20main,and%2042%25%20of%20children%20worldwide; https://www.stanfordchildrens.org/en/topic/default?id=diagnosing-anemia-in-children-161-1.

9. B Lozoff, E Jimenez, J Hagen, E Mollen, and AW Wolf, "Poorer Behavioral and Developmental Outcome More Than 10 Years After Treatment for Iron Deficiency in Infancy," *Pediatrics* 105, no. 4 (April 1, 2000): e51, https://doi.org/10.1542/peds.105.4.e51.

10. JT Cook and DA Frank. "Food Security, Poverty, and Human Development in the United States," *Annals of the New York Academy of Sciences* 1136, no. 1 (June 2008): 193–209, https://doi.org/10.1196/annals.1425.001.

11. R Molteni, RJ Barnard, Z Ying, CK Roberts, and F Gómez-Pinilla, "A High-Fat, Refined Sugar

Diet Reduces Hippocampal Brain-Derived Neurotrophic Factor, Neuronal Plasticity, and Learning," *Neuroscience* 112, no. 4 (2002): 803–814, https://doi.org/10.1016/s0306-4522(02)00123-9.

12. SS Morris, B Cogill, and R Uauy, "Effective International Action Against Undernutrition: Why Has It Proven So Difficult and What Can Be Done to Accelerate Progress?" *The Lancet* 371, no. 9612 (February 16, 2008): 608–621, https://doi.org/10.1016/S0140-6736(07)61695-X.

13. DB Jackson, "The Link Between Poor Quality Nutrition and Childhood Antisocial Behavior: A Genetically Informative Analysis," *Journal of Criminal Justice* 44, no. 2 (March 2016): 13–20, https://doi.org/10.1016/j.jcrimjus.2015.11.007.

14. DB Jackson, "Diet Quality and Bullying Among a Cross-National Sample of Youth," *Preventive Medicine* 105 (December 2017): 359–365, https://doi.org/10.1016/j.ypmed.2017.06.033.

15. JM Perkins, SV Subramanian, GD Smith, and E Özaltin, "Adult Height, Nutrition, and Population Health." *Nutrition Reviews* 74, no. 3 (March 2016): 149–165, https://doi.org/10.1093/nutrit/nuv105.

16. United Nations Department of Economic and Social Affairs, "End Hunger, Achieve Food Security and Improved Nutrition and Promote Sustainable Agriculture," https://sdgs.un.org/goals/goal2.

17. G Fink and PC Rockers, "Childhood Growth, Schooling, and Cognitive Development: Further Evidence from the Young Lives Study," *The American Journal of Clinical Nutrition* 100, no. 1 (May 7, 2014): 182–188, https://doi.org/10.3945/ajcn.113.080960.

18. RE Black, CG Victora, SP Walker, ZA Bhutta, P Christian, M de Onis, M Ezzati, S Grantha-McGregor, J Katz, R Martorell, et al, "Maternal and Child Undernutrition and Overweight in Low-Income and Middle-Income Countries," *The Lancet* 382, no. 9890 (August 3, 2013): 427–451, https://doi.org/10.1016/S0140-6736(13)60937-X.

19. J Mayneris-Perxachs and JR Swann, "Metabolic Phenotyping of Malnutrition During the First 1000 Days of Life," *European Journal of Nutrition* 58 (April 1, 2019): 909–930, https://doi.org/10.1007/s00394-018-1679-0.

20. "Adult Obesity Facts," Centers for Disease Control and Prevention, https://www.cdc.gov/obesity/data/adult.html.

21. JA Mennella and GK Beauchamp, "The Role of Early Life Experiences in Flavor Perception and Delight," in *Obesity Prevention*, eds. L Dube, A Bechara, A Dagher, A Drewnowski, J LeBel, P James, and RY Yada (London: Elsevier, 2010), 203–218.

22. M Yanina Pepino and JA Mennella, "Factors Contributing to Individual Differences in Sucrose Preference," *Chemical Senses* 30, suppl. 1 (January 2005): i319–i320, https://doi.org/10.1093/chemse/bjh243.

23. GK Beauchamp and K Engelman, "High Salt Intake: Sensory and Behavioral Factors," *Hypertension* 17, suppl. 1 (January 1, 1991): I176–I181, https://doi.org/10.1161/01.HYP.17.1_Suppl.I176.

24. JA Mennella, CP Jagnow, and GK Beauchamp, "Prenatal and Postnatal Flavor Learning by Human Infants," *Pediatrics* 107, no. 6 (June 1, 2001): e88, https://doi.org/10.1542/peds.107.6.e88.

25. PAS Breslin, "An Evolutionary Perspective on Food and Human Taste." *Current Biology* 23, no. 9 (May 6, 2013): R409–R418, https://doi.org/10.1016/j.cub.2013.04.010.

26. R Luoto, M Kalliomäki, K Laitinen, NM Delzenne, PD Cani, S Salminen, and E Isolauri, "Initial Dietary and Microbiological Environments Deviate in Normal-Weight Compared to Overweight Children at 10 Years of Age," *Journal of Pediatric Gastroenterology and Nutrition* 52, no. 1 (January 2011): 90–95, https://doi.org/10.1097/MPG.0b013e3181f3457f. M Kalliomäki, MC Collado, S Salminen, and E Isolauri, "Early Differences in Fecal Microbiota Composition in Children May Predict Overweight," *The American Journal of Clinical Nutrition* 87, no 3 (March 1, 2008): 534–538, https://doi.org/10.1093/ajcn/87.3.534.

27. RF Slykerman, J Thompson, KE Waldie, R Murphy, C Wall, and EA Mitchell, "Antibiotics in the First Year of Life and Subsequent Neurocognitive Outcomes," *Acta Paediatrica* 106, no. 1 (October 4, 2016): 87–94, https://doi.org/10.1111/apa.13613.

28. LM Cox and MJ Blaser, "Antibiotics in Early Life and Obesity," *Nature Reviews Endocrinology* 11, no. 3 (March 2015): 182–190, https://doi.org/10.1038/nrendo.2014.210.

29. SE Cusick and MK Georgieff, "The Role of Nutrition in Brain Development: The Golden Opportunity of the 'First 1000 Days,'" *The Journal of Pediatrics* 175 (June 3, 2016): 16–21, https://doi.org/10.1016/j.jpeds.2016.05.013.

CHAPTER 2

1. MA Kominiarek and P Rajan, "Nutrition Recommendations in Pregnancy and Lactation," *The Medical Clinics of North America* 100, no. 6 (November 2016): 1199–1215, https://doi.org/10.1016/j.mcna.2016.06.004.

2. KB Comerford, KT Ayoob, RD Murray, and SA Atkinson, "The Role of Avocados in Maternal Diets during the Periconceptional Period, Pregnancy, and Lactation, *Nutrients*, 8, no. 5 (May 21, 2016): 313, https://doi.org/10.3390/nu8050313.

3. Ibid.

4. HW Korsmo, J Xinyin, and MA Caudill, "Choline: Exploring the Growing Science on Its Benefits for Moms and Babies." *Nutrients* 11, no. 8 (August 7, 2019): 1823, https://doi.org/10.3390/nu11081823.

5. GM Shaw, RH Finnell, HJ Blom, SL Carmichael, SE Vollset, W Yang, and PM Ueland, "Choline and Risk of Neural Tube Defects in a Folate-Fortified Population," *Epidemiology* 20, no. 5 (September 2009): 714–719, https://doi.org/10.1097/EDE.0b013e3181ac9fe7.

6. FJK Toloza, H Motahari, and S Maraka, "Consequences of Severe Iodine Deficiency in Pregnancy: Evidence in Humans," *Frontiers in Endocrinology* 11 (June 19, 2020): 409. https:doi.org/10.3389/fendo.2020.00409.

7. M Makrides, RA Gibson, AJ McPhee, L Yelland, J Quinlivan, P Ryan, and DOMInO Investigative Team, "Effect of DHA Supplementation During Pregnancy on Maternal Depression and Neurodevelopment of Young Children: A Randomized Controlled Trial," *JAMA* 304, no. 15 (October 20, 2010): 1675–1683, https:doi.org/10.1001/jama.2010.1507.

8. S Bastos Maia, AS Rolland Souza, MdF Costa Caminha, S Lins da Silva, RdSBL Callou Cruz, C Carvalho dos Santos, and M Batista Filho, "Vitamin A and Pregnancy: A Narrative Review," *Nutrients* 11, no. 3 (March 22, 2019): 681, https://doi.org/10.3390/nu11030681.

9. P Gluckman, M Hanson, Y-S Chong, and A Bardsley, *Nutrition and Lifestyle for Pregnancy and Breastfeeding* (Oxford, England: Oxford University Press, 2015), https:doi.org/10.1093/med/9780198722700.001.0001.

10. S Barua, S Kuizon, and MA Junaid, "Folic Acid Supplementation in Pregnancy and Implications in Health and Disease," *Journal of Biomedical Science* 21, article 77 (August 19, 2014), https://doi.org/10.1186/s12929-014-0077-z.

11. RK Chandyo, M Ulak, I Kvestad, M Shrestha, S Ranjitkar, S Basnet, M Hysing, L Shrestha, and TA Strand, "The Effects of Vitamin B_{12} Supplementation in Pregnancy and Postpartum on Growth and Neurodevelopment in Early Childhood: Study Protocol for a Randomized Placebo Controlled Trial," *BMJ Open* 7 (2017): e016434, https://doi.org/10.1136/bmjopen-2017-016434.

12. JJ Otten, JP Hellwig, and LD Meyers, eds., *Dietary Reference Intakes: The Essential Guide to Nutrient Requirements* (Washington, DC: National Academies Press, 2006), https://doi.org/10.17226/11537.

13. Hippocrates, "On Ancient Medicine," *The Genuine Works of Hippocrates,* translated by Charles Darwin Adams, New York: Dover, 1868.

14. AF Dörsam, H Preißl, N Micali, SB Lörcher, S Zipfel, and KE Giel, "The Impact of Maternal Eating Disorders on Dietary Intake and Eating Patterns during Pregnancy: A Systematic Review," *Nutrients* 11, no. 4 (April 13, 2019); 840, https://doi.org/10.3390/nu11040840.

15. L Belbasis, MD Savvidou, C Kanu, E Evangelou, and I Tzoulaki, "Birth Weight in Relation to Health and Disease in Later Life: An Umbrella Review of Systematic Reviews and Meta-Analyses," *BMC Medicine* 14, article 147 (September 28, 2016), https://doi.org/10.1186/s12916-016-0692-5.

16. J Cerretani, "Targeting Childhood Obesity Early," *The Harvard Gazette,* September 18, 2012, https://news.harvard.edu/gazette/story/2012/09/targeting-childhood-obesity-early.

17. MI Goran, AA Martin, TL Alderete, H Fujiwara, and DA Fields, "Fructose in Breast Milk Is

Positively Associated with Infant Body Composition at 6 Months of Age," *Nutrients* 9, no. 2 (February 16, 2017): 146, https://doi.org/10.3390/nu9020146.

18. MB Azad, AK Sharma, RJ de Souza, VW Dolinsky, AB Becker, PJ Mandhane, SE Turvey, P Subbarao, DL Lefebvre, and MR Sears, "Association Between Artificially Sweetened Beverage Consumption During Pregnancy and Infant Body Mass Index," *JAMA Pediatrics* 170, no. 7 (July 2016): 662–670. https://doi.org/10.1001/jamapediatrics.2016.0301.

19. JA Mennella and GK Beauchamp, "Experience with a Flavor in Mother's Milk Modifies the Infant's Acceptance of Flavored Cereal," *Developmental Psychobiology* 35, no. 3 (November 1999): 197–203, https://doi.org/10.1002/(sici)1098-2302(199911)35:3<197::aid-dev4>3.0.co;2-j.

20. JA Mennella, A Johnson, and GK Beauchamp, "Garlic Ingestion by Pregnant Women Alters the Odor of Amniotic Fluid," *Chemical Senses* 20, no. 2 (April 1995): 207–209, https://doi.org/10.1093/chemse/20.2.207.

21. SP Walker, TD Wachs, JM Gardner, B Lozoff, GA Wasserman, E Pollitt, and JA Carter, "Child Development: Risk Factors for Adverse Outcomes in Developing Countries," *The Lancet* 369, no. 9556 (January 13, 2007):145–157, https://doi.org/10.1016/S0140-6736(07)60076-2.

22. P Łoboś and A Januszewicz, "Food Neophobia in Children." *Pediatric Endocrinology Diabetes and Metabolism* 25, no. 3, (March 2019): 150–154. https://doi.org/10.5114/pedm.2019.87711.

23. "Breastfeeding," World Health Organization, accessed August 8, 2018, http://www.who.int/nutrition/topics/exclusive_breastfeeding/en.

24. NM Frank, KF Lynch, U Uusitalo, J Yang, M Lönnrot, SM Virtanen, H Hyöty, and JM Norris, "The relationship between breastfeeding and reported respiratory and gastrointestinal infection rates in young children," *BMC Pediatrics* 19, article 339 (September 18, 2019), https://doi.org/10.1186/s12887-019-1693-2.

25. J Yan, et al, "The association between breastfeeding and childhood obesity: a meta-analysis," *BMC Public Health* 14, 1267 (December 2014), https://doi.org/10.1186/1471-2458-14-1267.

26. A Stuebe, "The Risks of Not Breastfeeding for Mothers and Infants," *Reviews in Obstetrics and Gynecology* 2, no. 4 (Fall 2009): 222–231, https://www.ncbi.nlm.nih.gov/pmc/articles/PMC2812877/.

27. "Maternal Diet," Centers for Disease Control and Prevention, last modified September 2, 2021, https://www.cdc.gov/breastfeeding/breastfeeding-special-circumstances/diet-and-micronutrients/maternal-diet.html.

28. P Salari and M Abdollahi, "The Influence of Pregnancy and Lactation on Maternal Bone Health: A Systematic Review," *Journal of Family & Reproductive Health* 8, no. 4 (December 2014): 135–148.

29. F Bravi, F Wiens, A Decarli, A Dal Pont, C Agostoni, and M Ferraroni, "Impact of Maternal Nutrition on Breast-Milk Composition: A Systematic Review," *The American Journal of Clinical Nutrition* 104, no. 3 (September 2016): 646–662, https://doi.org/10.3945/ajcn.115.120881.

30. Institute of Medicine (US) Committee on Nutritional Status During Pregnancy and Lactation, "6. Milk Composition," in *Nutrition During Lactation* (Washington, DC: National Academies Press, 1991), available from https://www.ncbi.nlm.nih.gov/books/NBK235590.

31. HB Clayton, et al, "Prevalence and Reasons for Introducing Infants Early to Solid Foods: Variations by Milk Feeding Type," *Pediatrics* 131, no. 4 (April 2013): e1108–1114, https://doi.org/10.1542/peds.2012-2265. AA Kuo, et al, "Introduction of Solid Food to Young Infants." *Maternal and Child Health Journal* 15, no. 8 (November 2011): 1185–1194, https://doi.org/10.1007/s10995-010-0669-5. SY Huh, et al, "Timing of Solid Food Introduction and Risk of Obesity in Preschool-Aged Children." *Pediatrics* 127, no. 3 (March 2011): e544–e551, https://doi.org/10.1542/peds.2010-0740.

32. https://healthychildren.org/English/ages-stages/baby/feeding-nutrition/Pages/Starting-Solid-Foods.aspx.

33. RE Kleinman, ed., *Pediatric Nutrition Handbook,* 6th ed. (Elk Grove Village, IL: American Academy of Pediatrics, 2008).

34. W Guo, et al, "Persistent Organic Pollutants in Food: Contamination Sources, Health Effects and Detection Methods." *International Journal of Environmental Research and Public Health* 16, no. 22 (November 2019): 4361, https://doi.org/10.3390/ijerph16224361.

35. WJ Crinnion, "Organic Foods Contain Higher Levels of Certain Nutrients, Lower Levels of Pesticides, and May Provide Health Benefits for the Consumer," *Alternative Medicine Review* 15, no 1 (April 1, 2010): 4–12, PMID: 20359265.

36. AD Dangour, K Lock, A Hayter, A Aikenhead, E Allen, and R Uauy, "Nutrition-Related Health Effects of Organic Foods: A Systemic Review," *American Journal of Clinical Nutrition* 92, no. 1 (July 2010): 203–210, https://doi.org/10.3945/ajcn.2010.29269.

37. E Palupi, A Jayanegara, A Ploegar, and J Kahl, "Comparison of Nutritional Quality Between Conventional and Organic Dairy Products: A Meta-Analysis," *Journal of the Science of Food and Agriculture* 92, no 14 (November 2012): 2774–2781, https://doi.org/10.1002/jsfa.5639.

38. US House of Representatives Committee on Oversight and Reform, *Baby Foods Are Tainted with Dangerous Levels of Arsenic, Lead, Cadmium, and Mercury,* February 4, 2021, https://oversight.house.gov/sites/democrats.oversight.house.gov/files/2021-02-04%20ECP%20Baby%20Food%20Staff%20Report.pdf.

39. https://www.healthybabyfood.org/sites/healthybabyfoods.org/files/2020-04/BabyFoodReport_ENGLISH_R6.pdf.

40. M Tolins, M Ruchirawat, and P Landrigan, "The Developmental Neurotoxicity of Arsenic: Cognitive and Behavioral Consequences of Early Life Exposure," *Annals of Global Health* 80, no. 4 (July–August 2014): 303–314, https://doi.org/10.1016/j.aogh.2014.09.005. CR Gale, et al, "The Influence of Head Growth in Fetal Life, Infancy, and Childhood on Intelligence at the Ages of 4 and 8 Years," *Pediatrics* 118, no 4 (October 2006): 1486–1492, https://doi.org/10.1542/peds.2005-2629.

41. P Grandjean and PJ Landrigan, "Neurobehavioural Effects of Developmental Toxicity," *Lancet Neurology* 13, no. 3 (March 2014): 330–338, https://doi.org/10.1016/S1474-4422(13)70278-3.

42. https://www.consumerreports.org/food-safety/heavy-metals-in-baby-food-a6772370847.

43. M Carey, et al, "Dilution of rice with other gluten free grains to lower inorganic arsenic in foods for young children in response to European Union regulations provides impetus to setting stricter standards." *PloS One* 13, no. 3 (March 2018): e0194700, https://doi.org/10.1371/journal.pone.0194700.

44. https://www.niehs.nih.gov/research/resources/articles_journals/bpa-related/index.cfm

45. JM Braun, AE Kalkbrenner, AM Calafat, K Yolton, X Ye, KN Dietrich, and BP Lanphear, "Impact of Early-Life Bisphenol A Exposure on Behavior and Executive Function in Children," *Pediatrics* 128, no. 5 (November 1, 2011): 873–882, https://doi.org/10.1542/peds.2011-1335.

46. https://www.ipsos-retailperformance.com/en/vegan-trends/.

47. NS Klimenko, AV Tyakht, AS Popenko, AS Vasiliev, IA Altukhov, DS Ischenko, TI Shashkova, DA Efimova, DA Nikogosov, DA Osipenko, et al, "Microbiome Responses to an Uncontrolled Short-Term Diet Intervention in the Frame of the Citizen Science Project," *Nutrients* 10, no. 5 (May 8, 2018), 576. https://doi.org/10.3390/nu10050576.

48. V Melina, W Craig, and S Levin, "Position of the Academy of Nutrition and Dietetics: Vegetarian Diets," *Journal of the Academy of Nutrition and Dietetics* 116, no. 12 (November 22, 2016): 1970–1980, https://doi.org/10.1016/j.jand.2016.09.025.

49. R Zimlich, "Plant-Based Protein Diets for Children," *Contemporary Pediatrics* 38, no. 4 (April 7, 2021), https://www.contemporarypediatrics.com/view/plant-based-protein-diets-for-children.

50. "The Nutrition Source – Protein," Harvard T.H. Chan School of Public Health, accessed April 6, 2021, https://www.hsph.harvard.edu/nutritionsource/what-should-you-eat/protein.

51. https://www.washingtonpost.com/opinions/we-need-a-war-on-secondhand-sugars/2017/01/27/1ad09020-d763-11e6-9a36-1d296534b31e_story.html.

52. M Goran and E Ventura, *Sugarproof: The Hidden Dangers of Sugar That Are Putting Your Child's Health at Risk and What You Can Do* (New York: Avery, 2020).

CHAPTER 3

1. JA Mennella, "Ontogeny of Taste Preferences: Basic Biology and Implications for Health," The American Journal of Clinical Nutrition 99, no. 3 (March 2014): 704S–711S, https://doi.org/10.3945/ajcn.113.067694.

2. PAS Breslin, "An Evolutionary Perspective on Food and Human Taste," *Current Biology* 23, no. 9 (May 6, 2013): R409–418, https://doi.org/10.1016/j.cub.2013.04.010.

3. JA Mennella and GK Beauchamp, "The Transfer of Alcohol to Human Milk: Effects on Flavor and the Infant's Behavior," *New England Journal of Medicine* 325 (October 3, 1991): 981–985, https://doi.org/10.1056/NEJM199110033251401.

4. JA Mennella and CJ Gerrish, "Effects of Exposure to Alcohol in Mother's Milk on Infant Sleep," *Pediatrics* 101, no. 5 (May 1, 1998): 21–25, https:doi.org/10.1542/peds.101.5.e2.

5. JA Mennella and GK Beauchamp, "The Infant's Response to Scented Toys: Effects of Exposure," *Chemical Senses* 23, no. 1 (1998): 11–17.

6. K Kähkönen, M Sandell, A Rönkä, M Hujo, and O Nuutinen, "Children's Fruit and Vegetable Preferences Are Associated with Their Mothers' and Fathers' Preferences," *Foods* 10, no. 2 (January 27, 2021): 261, https://doi.org/10.3390/foods10020261.

7. R Wyse, E Campbell, N Nathan, and L Wolfenden, "Associations Between Characteristics of the Home Food Environment and Fruit and Vegetable Intake in Preschool Children: A Cross-Sectional Study," *BMC Public Health* 11, article 938 (December 16, 2011), https://doi.org/10.1186/1471-2458-11-938.

8. GG Zeinstra, MA Koelen, FJ Kok, N van der Laan, and C de Graaf, "Parental Child-Feeding Strategies in Relation to Dutch Children's Fruit and Vegetable Intake," *Public Health Nutrition* 13 (September 22, 2009): 787–796, https://doi.org/10.1017/S1368980009991534.

9. CE Holley, C Farrow, and E Haycraft, "If at First You Don't Succeed: Assessing Influences Associated with Mothers' Reoffering of Vegetables to Preschool Age Children," *Appetite* 123 (April 1, 2018): 249–255, https://doi.org/10.1016/j.appet.2017.12.026.

10. KA Loth, M Horning, S Friend, D Neumark-Sztainer, and J Fulkerson, "An Exploration of How Family Dinners Are Served and How Service Style Is Associated with Dietary and Weight Outcomes in Children," *Journal of Nutrition Education and Behavior* 49, no. 6 (June 1, 2017): 513–518.E1, https://doi.org/10.1016/j.jneb.2017.03.003.

11. M Mura Paroche, SJ Caton, CMJL Vereijken, H Weenen, and C Houston-Price, "How Infants and Young Children Learn About Food: A Systematic Review." *Frontiers in Psychology* 8 (July 25, 2017): 1046, https://doi.org/10.3389/fpsyg.2017.01046.

12. N Rigal, C Chabanet, S Issanchou, and S Monnery-Patris, "Links Between Maternal Feeding Practices and Children's Eating Difficulties: Validation of French Tools," *Appetite* 58, no. 2 (April 2012): 629–637, https://doi.org/10.1016/j.appet.2011.12.016.

13. MD Patel, et al, "Considering Nature and Nurture in the Etiology and Prevention of Picky Eating: A Narrative Review," *Nutrients* 12, no. 11 (November 6, 2020): 3409, https://doi.org/10.3390/nu12113409.

14. AA Roess, EF Jacquier, DJ Catellier, R Carvalho, AC Lutes, AS Anater, WH Dietz, "Food Consumption Patterns of Infants and Toddlers: Findings from the Feeding Infants and Toddlers Study (FITS) 2016," *The Journal of Nutrition*, 148, suppl. 3 (September 2018): 1525S–1535S, https://doi.org/10.1093/jn/nxy171.

15. "Childhood Obesity Facts," Centers for Disease Control and Prevention, https://www.cdc.gov/obesity/data/childhood.html.

16. KM Flegal, MD Carroll, and BK Kit, "Prevalence of Obesity and Trends in the Distribution of Body Mass Index Among US Adults, 1999–2010," *JAMA* 307, no. 5 (2012): 491–497, https://doi.org/10.1001/jama.2012.39.

17. EM Steele, BM Popkin, B Swinburn, and CA Monteiro, "The Share of Ultra-Processed Foods and the Overall Nutritional Quality of Diets in the US: Evidence from a Nationally Representative Cross-Sectional Study," *Population Health Metrics* 15, article 6 (February 14, 2017), https://doi.org/10.1186/s12963-017-0119-3.

18. "Children's Cereals: Sugar by the Pound," Environmental Working Group, https://static.ewg.org/reports/2014/cereals/pdf/2014-EWG-Cereals-Report.pdf.

19. "Barbara's 2017 Breakfast Survey Reveals Parents Are Sacrificing Nutrition So Kids Will Eat Breakfast," *Business Wire*, https://www.businesswire.com/news/home/20170919005598/en/Barbara%E2%80%99s-2017-Breakfast-Survey-Reveals-Parents-Are-Sacrificing-Nutrition-So-Kids-Will-Eat-Breakfast.

20. L Cooke, S Carnell, and J Wardle, "Food Neophobia and Mealtime Food: Consumption in 4–5 Year Old Children," *International Journal of Behavioral Nutrition and Physical Activity* 3, article 14 (July 6, 2006), https://doi.org/10.1186/1479-5868-3-14.

21. GL Mitchell, C Farrow, E Haycraft, and C Meyer, "Parental Influences on Children's Eating Behaviour and Characteristics of Successful Parent-Focussed Interventions," *Appetite* 60, no. 1 (January 1, 2013): 85–94, https://doi.org/10.1016/j.appet.2012.09.014.

CHAPTER 4

1. JA Mennella, JM Kennedy, and GK Beauchamp, "Vegetable Acceptance by Infants: Effects of Formula Flavors," *Early Human Development* 82, no. 7 (July 2006): 463–468, https://doi.org/10.1016/j.earlhumdev.2005.12.001.

2. RW Salah, et al, "The Prevalence and Predictors of Iron Deficiency Anemia among Rural Infants in Nablus Governorate," *Journal of Research in Health Sciences* 18, no. 3 (June 13, 2018): e00417.

3. JK Bird, RA Murphy, ED Ciappio, and MI McBurney, "Risk of Deficiency in Multiple Concurrent Micronutrients in Children and Adults in the United States," *Nutrients* 9, no. 7 (June 24, 2017): 655, https://doi.org/10.3390/nu9070655.

4. N Singh, T Tripathi, P Rai, and P Gupta, "Nutrition and Orthodontics: Interdependence and Interrelationship," *Research & Reviews: Journal of Dental Sciences*. (September 2017).

5. Information for all daily recommended intake values are from the following sources: National Institute of Health: https://ods.od.nih.gov/factsheets/list-VitaminsMinerals; https://ods.od.nih.gov/HealthInformation/Dietary_Reference_Intakes.aspx; US Department of Agriculture and US Department of Health and Human Services, *Dietary Guidelines for Americans, 2020–2025*, 9th ed. (December 2020), available at dietaryguidelines.gov.

6. A Stephen, M Alles, C de Graaf, M Fleith, E Hadjilucas, E Isaacs, C Maffeis, G Zeinstra, C Matthys, and A Gil, "The Role and Requirements of Digestible Dietary Carbohydrates in Infants and Toddlers," *European Journal of Clinical Nutrition* 66, no. 7 (July 2012): 765–779, https://doi.org.10.1038/ejcn.2012.27.

7. A Hilbig and M Kersting, "Effects of Age and Time on Energy and Macronutrient Intake in German Infants and Young Children: Results of the DONALD Study," *Journal of Pediatric Gastroenterology and Nutrition* 43, no. 4 (October 2006): 518–524, https://doi.org/10.1097/01.mpg.0000229548.69702.aa.

8. K Sonneville, *Manual of Pediatric Nutrition*, 5th ed, Division of Adolescent and Young Adult Medicine, Boston Children's Hospital and Instructor, Harvard Medical School, Boston, Massachusetts, USA.

9. R Francavilla, et al, "Effect of Lactose on Gut Microbiota and Metabolome of Infants with Cow's Milk Allergy," *Pediatric Allergy and Immunology* 23, no. 5 (August 2012): 420–427, https://doi.org/10.1111/j.1399-3038.2012.01286.x.

10. NM Avena, P Rada, and BG Hoebel, "Evidence for Sugar Addiction: Behavioral and Neurochemical Effects of Intermittent, Excessive Sugar Intake," *Neuroscience and Biobehavioral Reviews* 32, no. 1 (2008): 20–39, https://doi.org/10.1016/j.neubiorev.2007.04.019.

11. SE Cusick and MK Georgieff, "The Role of Nutrition in Brain Development: The Golden Opportunity of the 'First 1000 Days,'" *The Journal of Pediatrics* 175 (2016): 16–21, https://doi.org/10.1016/j.jpeds.2016.05.013.

12. K Capone, S Sriram, T Patton, D Weinstein, E Newton, K Wroblewski, T Sentongo, "Effects of Chromium on Glucose Tolerance in Infants Receiving Parenteral Nutrition Therapy," *Nutrition in Clinical Practice* 33, no. 3 (June 2018): 426–432, https://doi.org/10.1177/0884533617711162.

13. RE Black, et al, "Maternal and Child Undernutrition and Overweight in Low-Income and Middle Income Countries." *The Lancet* 382, no. 9890 (August 2013): 427–51, https://doi.org/10.1016/S0140-6736(13)60937-X.

14. RA Jacob, "Folate and Choline Interplay Investigated," *Agricultural Research* 22, no. 1 (March 2001): 16–17.

15. GM Shaw, SL Carmichael, W Yang, S Selvin, and DM Schaffer, "Periconceptional Dietary Intake of Choline and Betaine and Neural Tube Defects in Offspring," *American Journal of Epidemiology* 160, no. 2 (July 15, 2004): 102–109, https://doi.org/10.1093/aje/kwh187.

16. DM Mock, "Biotin: From Nutrition to Therapeutics," in *Modern Nutrition in Health and Disease*, 11th ed., AC Ross, et al, eds., (Lippincott Williams & Wilkins, 2014): 390–398.

17. A Imdad, MY Yakoob, C Sudfeld, BA Haider, RE Black, and ZA Bhutta, "Impact of Vitamin A Supplementation on Infant and Childhood Mortality," *BMC Public Health* 11, suppl. 3 (April 13, 2011): S20, https://doi.org/10.1186/1471-2458-11-S3-S20.

18. "Beriberi," *Healthline*, accessed December 11, 2015, http://www.healthline.com/health/beriberi#Overview1.

19. LH Allen, "B Vitamins in Breast Milk: Relative Importance of Maternal Status and Intake, and Effects on Infant Status and Function," *Advances in Nutrition: An International Review Journal* 3, no. 3 (May 2012): 362–369, https://doi.org/10.3945/an.111.001172.

20. "Vitamin B$_5$," University of Maryland, accessed November 8, 2015, https://umm.edu/health/medical/altmed/supplement/vitamin-b5-pantothenic-acid.

21. SJ Fomon, "Infant Feeding in the 20th Century: Formula and Beikost," *The Journal of Nutrition* 131, no. 2 (February 2001): 409S–420S, https://doi.org/10.1093/jn/131.2.409S.

22. MM Black, "Micronutrient Deficiencies and Cognitive Functioning," *The Journal of Nutrition* 133, no. 11 (November 2003): 3927S–3931S, https://doi.org/10.1093/jn/133.11.3927S.

23. "Vitamin B-12," Mayo Clinic, accessed August 28, 2015, http://www.mayoclinic.org/drugs-supplements/vitamin-b12/dosing/hrb-20060243.

24. T Strand, S Taneja, T Kumar, MS Manger, H Refsum, CS Yajnik, and N Bhandari, "Vitamin B-12, Folic Acid, and Growth in 6- to 30-Month-Old Children: A Randomized Controlled Trial," *Pediatrics* 135, no. 4 (April 2015): e918–e926, https://doi.org/10.1542/peds.2014-1848.

25. R L Schleicher, M Carroll, ES Ford, and DA Lacher, "Serum Vitamin C and the Prevalence of Vitamin C Deficiency in the United States: 2003–2004 National Health and Nutrition Examination Survey (NHANES)," *The Journal of Nutrition* 90, no. 5 (November 2009): 1252–1263, https://doi.org/10.3945/ajcn.2008.27016.

26. J Bentley, "The Role of Vitamin D in Infants, Children and Young People," *Nursing Children and Young People* 27, no. 1 (February 2015): 28–35, https://doi.org/10.7748/ncyp.27.1.28.e508.

27. MB Zimmermann, et al, "Vitamin A Supplementation in Iodine-Deficient African Children Decreases Thyrotropin Stimulation of the Thyroid and Reduces the Goiter Rate," *The American Journal of Clinical Nutrition* 86, no. 4 (October 2007): 1040–1044, https://doi.org/10.1093/ajcn/86.4.1040. MB Zimmermann, "Interactions of Vitamin A and Iodine Deficiencies: Effects on the Pituitary-Thyroid Axis." *International Journal for Vitamin and Nutrition Research* 77, no. 3 (May 2007): 236–40, https://doi.org/10.1024/0300-9831.77.3.236.

28. L Chen, Y Zhu, Z Hu, S Wu, and C Jin. "Beetroot as a Functional Food with Huge Health Benefits: Antioxidant, Antitumor, Physical Function, and Chronic Metabolomics Activity." *Food Science & Nutrition* 9, no. 11 (November 2021): 6406–6420.

29. G-F Yuan, et al, "Effects of Different Cooking Methods on Health-Promoting Compounds of Broccoli," *Journal of Zhejiang University SCIENCE B* 10, no. 8 (August 2009): 580–588, https://doi.org/10.1631/jzus.B0920051.

CHAPTER 8

1. KN Jallad, "Heavy Metal Exposure from Ingesting Rice and Its Related Potential Hazardous Health Risks to Humans," *Environmental Science and Pollution Research International* 22, no. 20 (October 2015): 15449–15458, https://doi.org/10.1007/s11356-015-4753-7. https://www.consumerreports.org/cro/magazine/2015/01/how-much-arsenic-is-in-your-rice/index.htm.

Index

Page numbers in **bold** indicate illustrations.